TRANSCENDING THE HERO REINVENTING THE HEROIC

An Essay on André Gide's Theater

E. San Juan, Jr.
The University of Connecticut

UNIVERSITY
PRESS OF
AMERICA

Lanham • New York • London

Copyright © 1988 by

University Press of America,® Inc.

4720 Boston Way
Lanham, MD 20706

3 Henrietta Street
London WC2E 8LU England

British Cataloging in Publication Information Available

Library of Congress Cataloging-in-Publication Data

San Juan, E. (Epifanio), 1938-
Transcending the hero, reinventing the heroic.

Includes bibliographies.
1. Gide, Andrew, 1869-1951—Dramatic works.

2. Heroes in literature.   3. Courage in literature.
4. Mythology, Greek, in literature.   5. Bible in
literature.   I. Title.
PQ2613.I2Z668   1987   842'.912   87-21567
ISBN 0-8191-6632-4 (alk. paper)

All University Press of America books are produced on acid-free
paper which exceeds the minimum standards set by the National
Historical Publication and Records Commission.

For Karin and Eric

ACKNOWLEDGMENTS

I wish to thank the Research Council of the University of Connecticut, particularly Dean Thomas Giolas and the Foundation staff, for support in the preparation of the manuscript and for previous faculty research grants.

Early versions of parts of this book appeared in *Modern Drama, American Educational Theater Journal, Saint Louis University Quarterly, Discourse;* and in the anthology *Oedipus: Myth and Dramatic Form* edited by J. Sanderson and E. Zimmerman.

I am indebted to the following colleagues and friends who have given useful suggestions and advice on various occasions: Roger Bresnahan, Sam Noumoff, Doug Allen, John Beverley, Bruce Franklin, Fredric Jameson, Matthew Proser, Herbert Goldstone, Judith Doyle, and Alexander Taylor. Delia D. Aguilar provided as usual the necessary encouragement and criticism for this project.

Storrs, Connecticut, June 1987

CONTENTS

Except a grain of wheat fall into the ground and die, it abideth alone; but if it die, it bringeth forth much fruit.

—JOHN 12:24

Without Contraries is no progression . . . . .Energy is Eternal Delight . . . . Exuberance is beauty.

—WILLIAM BLAKE

. . . as for the game I was playing, I have won it . . . . I have said more or less what I had to say . . . .

It is in ourselves, in ourselves alone, that we must seek and find recourse. And should a little pride enter into this, is it not legitimate? For the sake of the austere and noble feeling of duty worthily accomplished, of the restoration in oneself of human potentiality?

—ANDRE GIDE

But by my love and hope I beseech you: do not throw away the hero in your soul! Hold holy your highest hope! . . . .

The most beautiful life, for a hero, is to ripen for a warrior's death.

—FRIEDRICH NIETZSCHE

INTRODUCTION

In the postmodernist context of decentered sensibilities, parodied gestures and transvalued selves, André Gide's writings, once outrageously innovative and nonconformist in his time, now seem a model of consistency and virtue. The artist of the perverse and the experimental now appears the paragon of modernist inwardness quite acceptable to the Establishment. The author of *The Counterfeiters* and *Lafcadio's Adventures* has been enshrined in the pantheon of culture as the exemplar of the artistic conscience upholding freedom and integrity. A felicitous irony or a gratuitous paradox?

Particularly in the light of his contribution to the famous volume *The God That Failed* (1950), his eloquent testimony of disillusionment at the socialist project he saw in the Soviet Union—a pastiche of impressions organized by the scholar Enid Starkie—has presented us Gide in the role of spokesman of "truth" and "the sanctity of the human soul." On the other hand, faithful to his principle of internal heterogeneity—"I allow all contradictions free play in me"—which, I submit, serves as the energizing motivation of his dramatic works surveyed here, he denounced the re-establishment of the "same old capitalist society" in the Soviet Union. Seeking salvation, Gide found not a utopia but a deceptive image of what he sought to flee: repressive Puritan conformity, bourgeois privileges, "the favoritism of inheritance and the whole procession of errors of capitalism to which our western world is still attached and which are dragging it headlong to its ruin."[1]

Gide's individualism has become paradigmatic, all too visibly inscribed in his artistic style, character system, and narrative strategy. His endeavor to invent a "Communist individualism" becomes a metaphor for his Nietzschean drive to fuse antitheses and synthesize contradictions. This drive to produce the unique, to constitute the idiosyncratic, may be traced to sources in the secular humanism of Renaissance thought (Montaigne) and the Reformation; but its immediate provenance seems to be a dissenting Protestant tradition that coalesces Montaigne and Pascal and generates a sensibility that seeks to blend the egocentric virtuosity of Rousseau and the haunted anguish of Dostoevsky's existential underground protagonist. In his autobiography, Gide identifies the religious root of his antinomian mode of critical judgement: "I began to feel that perhaps all men's obligations were not the same, and that God himself might well abhor the uniformity against which nature protests but towards which the Christian ideal seems to lead us in aiming to bring nature under control. I could concede none but an individual morality, its imperatives sometimes in conflict with those of other moralities. I was persuaded that each person, or at least one of the elect, had to play a role on earth, which was wholly his own and did not resemble any other. And every attempt to submit to a general rule became treason in my eyes, yes, treason which I likened to that great unpardonable sin against the Holy Ghost, since the individual lost his precise, irreplaceable significance, his savour."[2]

Why is the pursuit of individuality so obsessive in Gide's aesthetic? Given the emergence of global monopoly capitalism or imperialism at the turn of the century, and the thoroughgoing transformation of everything to commodities (exchange-values circulating in the "free market"), we no longer live in the *laissez-faire* stage of industrial society when the concept of individual rights in the social-political sphere was first theorized. Anomie in mass society and consumerism have intensified since the seventeeth century. Liberal individualism as argued by Locke and early social-contract philosophers then was premised on the idea that the state is but a system of constraints limiting the activities of the individual in order to protect his freedoms and rights, society being defined as a voluntary association of individuals. Gide agrees with this notion: the individual's rights and needs take precedence over all collectives in the making of moral and political decisions. However, while giving priority to the natural rights of individuals over against family, corporation, civil society, and the state, Gide does not fully concur with the anarchist-oriented individualism of recent thinkers (Nozick, Rawls) nor with the reductionist tendency that, from a metaphysical point of view, the individual can be conceived as an intelligible and self-sufficient entity apart from any social arrangement where she may be inserted. Gide seems to believe not so much in the atomized or monadic individual floating in a vacuum but in the human person whose essence is social. Individual persons can be understood only with reference to the social and institutional contexts of which they are microcosms, and in which they participate. Just as organisms are not aggregates of cells but form dynamic wholes, institutions cannot be reduced simply to aggregates of individuals. Invoking variations in nature and the mediation of the "Holy Spirit", Gide recognizes the notion of *species-being* (*Gattungswesen*) signifying that humans cannot be isolated from the existing social relations which constitute them as persons in their historically specific times and places.

Contraposed to the liberal Enlightenment doctrine of the primacy of the autonomous individual, Gide's individualism is intrinsically dialectical: the artist's mind is the site of struggle between impulses of classicism and romanticism. Gide emphasizes this agonistic process of creation: "And the work of art must be born from this struggle; the classical work of art tells of the triumph of order and measure over inner romanticism." [3] Classicism, for Gide, implies the triumph of individualism realized paradoxically in "the renunciation of individuality." Self-indulgence and mannerism suppress true individuality attained when the artist "strives for the commonplace." Gide elaborates in effect his ironic thesis of anti-individualism:

> A great artist has but one concern: to become as human as possible—or, to put it better, to be *commonplace*. . . . The wonderful thing is that he thus becomes more personal. But

he who flees humanity for himself alone, succeeds only in becoming special, bizarre, incomplete. It is perhaps appropriate to recall the words of the Gospel here — I do not think I am distorting the sense: "Whosoever shall seek to save his life shall lose it; and whosoever shall lose his life shall preserve it." (Or, to translate more faithfully the Greek text: ". . . . shall make it truly alive.")[4]

Gide's vision that the personal can be fully unfolded and concretized in the social or communal, in *species-being*, may be one logical consequence of his dialectical will to grasp paradoxes in everything, to pursue the motion of signifiers as a circular or spiral process, as evidenced in the following aphorisms: "Every affirmation ends up in abnegation . . . . Everything that strives to affirm itself negates itself; everything that renounces itself asserts itself. Complete possession is proved only by giving. All you are unable to give possesses you. Without sacrifice there is no resurrection."[5] In this context, the terms "individual" and "society" are not irreconcilable opposites but poles in a dynamic continuum, reciprocally and mutually interacting, capable of being finally apprehended in a totalizing imagination.

We can now appreciate Gide's individualism as a heightened self-awareness of positions (roles, beliefs, judgements) as moments in a constantly shifting process of mapping the space for the exploratory, protean imagination. This space assumes a theatrical or histrionic configuration: "What is called 'objectivity' today is easy for novelists devoid of inner landscape. I can state that I am interested, not in myself, but in the conflict of certain ideas of which my soul is the stage and in which I play the part less of an actor than of a spectator, a witness."[6] In a sense, all of Gide's plays may be construed as the allegorical choreography of ideas none of which have a central or primordial authority. He seeks to thwart the habitual need to fix meanings, to hypostatize the link between signifier and signified: "Because it has always been easier for me to choose and to reject in the name of someone else than in my own name, and because I always feel I am impoverishing myself when I limit myself, I am quite willing to have no well-defined existence if the individuals I create and draw from myself have one."[7] Gide aspires to disperse any stable or coherent ego identical with any moment of his consciousness; he dissociates himself perpetually from any self-presence or identity centered in any static or frozen quality or attribute. He privileges the process of playing off various positions simultaneously against each other:

> Nothing is accomplished if I have not truly been able to become this character that I am creating, and to depersonalize myself in him to the extent of being blamed for never having managed to portray anyone but myself — however different from one another may be Saül, Candaules, Alissa, Lafcadio, the minister of my *Symphonie pastorale*, or LaPérouse or Armand. It is returning to myself that embarrasses me, for, in truth, I no longer really know *who* I am; or, if you prefer, I never am; I am becoming.[8]

If character, for Gide, is only a moment in the manifestation of an inexhaustible reservoir of possibilities, then is it meaningful to expect Gide to entertain the notion of a hero or a heroic role?

Gide's use of Greek mythology and Biblical legends in his plays may be one mode of pursuing the theme Edouard (in *The Counterfeiters*) considers the "deep-lying subject" of his work: "the rivalry between the real world and the representation of it which we make to ourselves."[9] It is, in other words, the conflict between what reality offers and what we desire to make of it. Mythology offers Gide the easily accessible solution to his demand that the artist should "never present *ideas* except in terms of temperament and characters."[10] In his essay "Thoughts on Greek Mythology," Gide emphasizes the "reasonableness" of Greek myths in revealing the "psychological fatality," not the providential fate, which made the legendary heroes truthful and plausible representations. While Gide defines the heroic as the working out of an "inner fatality" in the protagonists, he singles out Hercules as "the only moral hero of antiquity" because his birth required the use of craft and deception when Jupiter succeeded in possessing the virtuous Alcmene. The heroic thus inheres in the experience of moral choice.

In the classical tradition, the hero personifies the collective virtues of superhuman strength, courage, moral integrity, and self-sacrifice. But with the disintegration of the unified world of tribal and feudal periods in society, the notion of the heroic has entered an ambiguous and problematic twilight region particularly when the romantic inflection of the heroic protagonist—the romantic interpretation of Satan as the hero of Milton's *Paradise Lost*, for example—testified to the exaltation of radical individualism against the communal values one may still find in the novels of Walter Scott or Jane Austen. In spite of the glorification of the anti-social rebel (Faust, Don Juan), the notion of the heroic suffered catastrophic erosion in the nineteenth-century validation of social-Darwinist and scientistic standards explaining human motivation, leading to the emergence of the absurd or villainous anti-hero now exemplified in the works of Beckett or Borges. It may be that the anti-hero of modernism inverts but does not banish the classical archetype: he becomes the ironic, intensely self-conscious, mocking and self-deprecating Zarathustra in a world where god has died. The hero then simply assumes other masks or personae appropriate to the demands of the situation, becoming the "intellectual hero," the middling or mediocre hero, the existential or unheroic hero, changing or metamorphosing as a function of the socio-historical contexts and the lived experience of various communities or groups.

In general, Gide subscribes to this modernist attitude of perspectival variation, the act of varying and substituting becoming the emblem of his unconventional "deconstructive" idiom. Roland Barthes captures precisely the fundamental thrust of Gide's imagination when he says that Gide "puts everything in the *movement* of his thought and not in its brutal profession." The adventure of a "conscience which honestly pursues its truth" springs from the following premises: "(1) the impulses of a soul are the mark of its authenticity (Gide's entire effort is to render himself and others 'authentic'); (2) the aesthetic pleasure he takes in slowly revealing the infinitesimal changes of his nature (*movement* remaining for Gide the best of man); (3) the profusion of his scruples in the search for truth, pursued through the finest nuances (truth is never brutal); (4) lastly, the moral importance accorded to states of conflict, perhaps because they are warrants of humility."[11] In quest of the authentic, Gide has always positioned himself at the intersection of the Greek and Christian roads—a "heroic situation"—where he is "protected by nothing but also enclosed by nothing." At the same time, Barthes insists that the fountainhead of Gide's art lies in the evangelical aphorism: "He who loveth his life shall lose it," on which a whole mythology of pride is erected.

To illustrate the operation of this idiosyncratic pride as the cardinal moral phenomenon distinguishing the authentic hero, authenticity being a function of the social context where the conflicted conscience can exhaust its possibilities, consider Gide's magnificent retelling of the parable of the prodigal son in Luke 15: 11-22, "The Return of the Prodigal Son."[12] At the outset, the narrator identifies himself openly with the prodigal son who, in remembering images of his past with his parents and somewhat falling "out of love with himself," returns as though submitting to a wager. Besieged by the ennui of his present, the future hypothetical situation of how he should respond to his father welcoming him back tempts the son. He imagines this situation and succumbs to the challenge.

Thwarting any fixed point of view, Gide anticipates what's going to happen, thus frustrating any suspense and generating an effect akin to Brecht's *Verfremdung-effekt*: even as the father and son are preparing their reprimands, we are told of a younger brother already stirring, dissatisfied, a replica of the prodigal son in the process of taking off. When the first panel of the triptych is unfolded, we see the astonishing dialectic of feeling displayed: in destitution and absence, love blossomed and he felt closer to his father. With the memory of his pleasure, the prodigal son cries of his yearning for "the wild taste of sweet acorns." A reversal suddenly intervenes when the father confesses: "It was I who made you. I know what is in you. I know what sent you out on your wanderings.

I was waiting for you at the end of the road. If you had called me . . . I was there." It is the Father then who affirms the worth of the son's refusal, valorizing the need to pursue "fervor," "the love which consumes. . . ."

In the second scene, the prodigal son voices his will to explore and experiment, to unbridle and indulge his "pride" rather than conform to "order": "I felt too clearly that the house is not the entire universe . . . . I could not help imagining other cultures, other lands, and roads by which to reach them, roads not yet traced. I imagined in myself the new being which I felt rushing down those roads. I ran away." The older brother easily stands for order, discipline, property, tradition. But when the prodigal son talks to his mother, he confesses: "Nothing is more fatiguing than to realize one's difference." He seeks the ' pleasure of returning to that condition which triggered his revolt; he renounces "the pride" which precipitated the rupture from his mother. Yet it is the mother who assays and validates the prodigal's impulse of negation when she points out the resemblance between him and his younger brother. She foresees the doubling of his self-serving act of liberation: "One day he will escape from me, I am sure."

Unfolding a panel that goes beyond the triptych, Gide now discloses that multi-layered complexity of motivation which Martin Turnell finds exactly registered in this subtly undermined parable.[13] The prodigal's dialectical arabesques become sheer exhibition of *disponibilité*. Incandescent gusto for excess and the susceptibility to denude the psyche coalesce here. While he explains to his younger brother that he left because he "felt duty-bound," immediately he qualifies that claim by declaring: "my weak reason let itself be conquered by my desires." But this rationalization quickly disappears when he asserts that he was looking for freedom—but only to be overwhelmed by doubts, "doubts about everything, about myself." Eventually, asked by his younger brother what he was looking for in the desert, the prodigal replies: "I myself do not understand now." We arrive at an empty space, a void waiting to be filled: the absolute, ineluctable rupture which, in post-structuralist thought, founds difference and the interminable

xviii

dance of signifiers. But it is not so much nihilistic freedom nor any tangible yield of pleasure in exploring the unknown that the prodigal seeks; he is looking for the "thirst" in the desert, "A thirst which that sour fruit alone can quench"—referring to the sour pomegranate the swineherd gave to the younger brother. By this metonymic placing of the fruit (icon of an unquenchable thirst for life, for wild uncharted space) inside the patriarchal house construed as a circumscribing law, taboo, or fetish, the narrative locates the internal self-contradiction of the prodigal: his gesture of finally recognizing his intimate fraternity with his kin signals the self-division of a temporary unity (the prodigal defined by the familial/patriarchal code), releasing the negative or creative element and identifying it with the younger brother. His parting words precisely encapsulate Gide's dialectics of heroic individualism:

> Leave me! leave me! I am staying to console our mother. Without me you will be braver. It is time now. The sky turns pale. Go without making any noise. Come! kiss me, my young brother, you are taking with you all my hopes. Be strong. Forget us. Forget me. May you never come back. . . . Go down quietly. I am holding the lamp. . . .

Foregoing whatever political resonance and implication this prose poem may have for the European milieu of 1907, I would simply emphasize here its archetypal import, its function as a model of Gide's maneuvers to invent the heroic as essentially the transcending of codes and boundaries, the valorization of the necessity to rebel as an *a priori* premise for any new conceptualization of the heroic.[14]

My reading of Gide's plays with deliberate focus on this thematic argument should be approached in the light of Gide's project sketched above, a project indissociable from his unique sensibility and the exemplary value of his commitments. The fundamental tension of Gide's life embodied in art is perspicuously summed up by Jean Paul Sartre as a relentless play of counterbalances between courage and prudence of which his theater is one expression: "Gide's art aims to establish a compromise between risk and rule, in him are balanced Protestant law and nonconformity of the homosexual, the arrogant individualism of the rich bourgeois, and the puritan taste for social restraint, a certain dryness, a difficulty in communicating, and a humanism which is Christian in origin, a strong sensuality which would like to be innocent; observance of the rule is united in him with the quest for spontaneity."[15]

---

[1] Richard H. Crossman, ed.,*The God that Failed* (New York, 1950), p. 50. For Gide's humanist communism, see Georges Brachfeld, *André Gide and the Communist Temptation* (Paris, 1959).

[2] Quoted in Kenneth Burke,*Counter-Statement* (Berkeley, 1968), p. 100.

[3] André Gide,*Pretexts: Reflections on Literature and Morality* (New York, 1959), p. 195.

[4] *Ibid.*, p. 197.

[5] *Ibid.*, p. 310.

[6] *Ibid.*, p. 307.

[7] *Ibid.*, p. 322.

[8] *Ibid.*, p. 323.

[9] *Ibid.*, p. 205.

[10] *Ibid.*, p. 406.

[11] Roland Barthes, *A Barthes Reader* (New York, 1982), p. 8.

[12] "The Return of the Prodigal Son," translated by Wallace Fowlie, in Maynard Mack, ed., *The Norton Anthology of World Masterpieces* (New York, 1970), pp. 1371-1384. All quotations are from this edition.

[13] Martin Turnell, *The Art of French Fiction* (New York, 1959), pp. 223-224, 283-284.

[14] For a biographically-oriented study of the text's genesis, see the interesting monograph by Aldyth Thain, *André Gide's The Return of the Prodigal Son* (Logan, Utah, 1960). It is possible to produce a reading of Gide's text as an illustration of one central thesis in the philosophy of the Italian Marxist philosopher Antonio Gramsci: "Each individual is not only the synthesis of existing relations, but also the history of those relations, the sum of all the past": *Selections from Prison Notebooks* (New York, 1971), p. 78.

[15] *Situations* (New York, 1966), p. 51. Compare the analysis of antithetical traits in Gide by Klaus Mann, *André Gide and the Crisis of Modern Thought* (New York, 1943), pp. 200-229.

I

IN QUEST OF THE HEROIC IN MODERN THEATER

A criticism of André Gide's dramatic works, if it seeks to be thorough and comprehensive, should not ignore Gide's aesthetic principles in the art of the theater. Formal and technical analysis must reckon with the universal implications of his ideas on which rest the significance and complexity of the dramatic works. Indeed, Gide the man and thinker cannot be isolated from Gide the dramatist. True, the integrity or the organic unity of each play can be primarily ascertained by an examination of the action and the character development, the interaction and interweaving of these two elements in the play. Yet action implies value; value in turn involves life and man in the world. Especially in the case of Gide, a purely literary criterion for judgment will prove too limited; soon, the critic discovers his method to be quite exclusive and academic.

Now Gide has openly expressed the moral direction of his theater on more than one occasion. To be sure, he never adhered to an esoteric kind of individualism for pleasure or for art's sake. The essential character of all his major writings, its basic orientation, is a moral one. For Gide aspired to communicate a way of life for each individual. And this way of life demands from each, as Gide exacted from himself in his lifetime, the realization of gifts hitherto intuited only as possibilities. He proposed: "Our value consists only in that which distinguishes us from others; our idiosyncracy is the sickness that gives us value."[1] This idea pervades Gide's essay,

1

"The Evolution of the Theater," in which he outlines more or less the intentions of his plays.

First of all, Gide imposed on the theater the task of a radical transvaluation. He decries the contemporary trend of the French theater as a trivial mimicry of social conventions. To designate the types of drama that strive to copy actual everyday life, he coins the term "episodic." What afflicts the theater today, says Gide, is precisely its paltry realism. Hopelessly paralyzed in conforming to what is normal, the theater ceases to be a moral force. Since all the barriers between actor and spectator have been abolished, one can no longer make distinctions between any two modes of being. Social habits in life become, in the realm of the theater, the convention which dominates the play and its actors. In this way public morality, through the agency of the realistic play, encroaches upon the stage, enervating the strength of its idealizing spirit.

Quoting Balzac's epigram that "morals are the hypocrisy of nations," Gide declares that the theater today has forfeited its old privilege of providing the audience ideal examples of character. The proper function of the theater is to create exalted models of humanity. It must inspire men to draw out of themselves their own hidden personalities, to develop their own native resources. Consequently, Gide contends that there is a need to react against realism if we would restore to the theater the role of challenging man to fulfill himself. For the common aim of most realistic plays is simply to entertain present-day society with what it likes and approves of; in short, to flatter the audience. In effect, the theater has been reduced to the duty of justifying the *status quo*. Ultimately the playwright becomes an apologist for his work.

Now Gide intends to restore to the theater its original task. He identifies his main intentions with that of Greek drama; hence his theater evolves from the tragedy of classical antiquity. From this viewpoint, Gide elects two modes of accomplishing the rebirth of the theater: first, he affirms the Greek conception of each man's uniqueness; secondly, pursuing the Greek conception of man, he advocates the adoption of certain theatrical conventions. How does Gide interpret the Greek conception of man's individuality? What are the conventions he wants the theater to follow?

Above all Gide's theater concerns itself with the search of the individual for self-fulfillment. He who is engaged in this search is the hero-protagonist. The essence of this humanistic approach may be found in the statement: "All things have always existed in man, sometimes seen, more or less, and sometimes hidden; what in recent times has been discovered in him is merely disclosed to sight but had been there asleep in man from the beginning.'[2] In man then resides everything conceivable. Gide's principle assumes too that each one is a fountain-head of all appearances, that each bears within himself the measure of his worth. Where in man specifically? In his desires. One's desires, so long as they rule one's actions, are the only true gods. Despotic reason falsifies desires and misleads the individual. To follow one's desire is to realize one's virtues. What Christianity regards as qualities of the soul, e.g. courage, goodness, etc., are simply the natural properties of the body. Thus, "the ideal type of man was not one but legion—or rather, there was no type of ideal man."[3]

There are as many gods as there are desires mastering the individual; hence, the Greek pantheon. Man serves these gods, these passions, in himself first before he projects his faith onto the skies; that is, monotheism exists in man first before it becomes a metaphysics. Interpreting classical ethics in terms of human psychology, Gide believes that man cannot become other than what he is. "What he is" signifies his desires, the whole temperament or disposition of his personality. To obey one's temperament is to realize one's true character. To Gide drama is fundamentally sustained by passion; and since passion stems from character, drama is nothing else but character. Consequently, he repudiates the tragedy of situations, of realistic or progressive "episodicism." Tragedy cannot live without the presence of exemplary characters. Character, in furnishing the initial motivation, makes dramatic action possible.

In our present Christian society, it is quite impossible to have such noble personages who exemplify (as they did

3

once in Machiavelli's time, for example) greatness of soul, bodily strength, and audacity through their deeds. Gide contends that the standard of Christian morality hampers, if not prevents, the development of personal character. This is because Christianity proposes to all men a common ideal: the imitation of Christ. He adds: "The soul demands heroism; but our present society barely leaves room for one form of heroism (if it even is heroism)—that of resignation, acceptance." Moreover, is it intelligible to conceive of tragedy, in the Sophoclean sense, whose last act is played out in the afterlife? Gide argues that Christian tragedy is not possible because "the last act must of necessity always take place in the wings—I mean in the other life." In the perspective of paganism, where the essence of man lies within himself, tragedy presents self-fulfillment as the identity between the individual and his deeds. For the individual to possess "character" in drama, his deeds have to be expressive of his ruling passions. In Gide's play we encounter characters with an unlimited variety of aspects. For example, when Philoctetes says, "To whom would I need to appear what I am? My only care is to be," he is illustrating Gide's theory that "for men whose desires are conquerors it is not hard to believe in the gods. It is not by free choice that man devoted himself to a particular god; the god recognized his own image in the man." To deliver this distinction between appearance and reality is the theater's main responsibility.

In what way could this responsibility be fulfilled? In our time, when hypocrisy dictates the reasons for action, there is every cause to expect from the theater a liberation from the tyranny of custom over nature. But the present situation is disappointing. The mask, which used to be worn by actors when life was spontaneous and natural, is now the property of the audience. Instead of exhibiting exemplary characters, the spectacle on the stage only reflects what everyone approves of: the average and ordinary. How can the theater offer a challenge to heroism when society can tolerate only its own habits, can sanction only the representation of its own manners? This, Gide points out, is exactly the dilemma confronting the theater today.

Gide asserts that the playwright, in order to regenerate the theater, must people the stage with heroic characters. But today you cannot draw exemplary characters from actual life, for everyone wills his own slavery to society. One must then separate the drama from actual life and the episodic. To do this would require the rediscovery of restrictions in certain theatrical conventions, for "art is born of constraint, thrives on struggle, dies of freedom." To Gide theatrical conventions are artistic modes which give birth to beauty by virtue of the constraint they impose upon the artist. He cites the case of the Shakespearean sonnet and Bach's fugue as fixed forms in which genius thrives most effectively. Dante's *terza rima* and Aeschylus' invention of dramatic silence (due to the traditional limitation of the number of voices on the stage) provide other edifying instances.[4]

The main objective of Gide in arguing for conventions is to create a gulf, a distance between the audience and the figures on the stage. In this connection, he endorses Racine's view that tragic characters must be regarded differently from the persons with whom one associates in real life. Thus, "the artist's choice of figures at a distance from us is due to the fact that time, or any kind of distance, allows only that image to supervene from which everything episodic, bizarre, and transitory has been refined away, so that what subsists is only that portion of deep truth with which art can do its work." In other words, drama must display the pure heroic action in all its classical simplicity. Only the heroic life, with its archetypal structure, can stimulate the individual to discover, not to form, what lies hidden in himself. Heroic characters in drama exist as provocations for us to realize our possibilities. Therefore one must not require the actors to be natural since they must move according to the particular laws of dramatic art. Gide's *Saul* and *Oedipus* may be envisaged as imitations of a serious action. It is an action in which the hero's character is revealed within the limits of the dramatic form.

Like meter in poetry, theatrical conventions are employed to create a system of expectation and fulfillment. Moreover, they establish an atmosphere of remoteness in time. Temporal distance enables the playwright, by exhibiting new forms of heroism, to defy the hypocrisy of custom and morals. In the context of the plays, heroism may be defined as the individual's struggle to discover his identity by following his own temperament. For this purpose Gide appropriates historical personages and mythical figures. Actually this borrowing or adaptation is only a device for creating aesthetic distance. Gide explains: "Properly speaking, there are no historical characters in poetry; only, when the poet wants to represent the world that he has conceived, he does certain individuals whom he encountered in history the honor of borrowing their names in order to attach them to the beings he has created." Further, Gide contends that the constraint offered by certain restrictions allows freedom to the artist to the extent that, within a limited field, he can explore the maximum of human potentialities. Beauty is born out of constraint, *la contrainte:* "Is it not in periods when life is most overflowing that the need of the strictest forms torment our most moving geniuses?" Facts must be distilled and concentrated under the control of a preconceived idea of beauty." In short, Gide strives for the Greek simplicity of dramatic action which we find, for instance, in Sophocles' *Oedipus Rex.* If the theater is able, by these means, to give voice to what is stifled in us by social routine, then it shall have performed its task of making us know who, and become what, we really are.

Gide's theater is then the theater of the individual struggling to find his own identity. In this struggle he becomes heroic. "We live in order to manifest," writes Gide in "Narcissus." [5] With this moral orientation (and "moral" should be construed in the light of the renaissance tradition of Montaigne), Gide's aesthetics invest his drama with a prophetic tone of address. As a "criticism of life," his drama evolves as a confrontation of the human condition. Insofar as it is a reaction against society, Gide's theater is also a reading and criticism of our own milieu. Premised on a certain interpretation of life's meaning, his theater contrives solutions to the major moral problems that beset the theater today. On the whole, Gide conceived of the theater as a medium for integrating the chaotic elements of modern

6

consciousness. Few can refuse to heed the importance of Gide's attempts to define the essence of man in his plays.

Since Gide views the theater as a moral agent, he adopts a subjective approach to the drama, an essentially objective literary form. Objective circumstances and characters are used to embody or symbolize the inner dialogue of opposing moral values: the sensual, dionysian and diabolic potencies of humans against the abstract god of his conscience. As a creature of dialogue, Gide recognized that only in the inner dialectic of fundamental extremes can one attain psychic balance or self-integration. In fact he considered himself born between two stars, arising out of the conflict between his father's southern Huguenot temperament and his mother's Roman Catholic faith. Manifest in the opposition between his puritan and his pagan emotions, this personal duality of motivation testifies to the complexity of the moral and philosophical development of Gide's thought and experience, of his evolving personality. Indeed, Gide's personality can be defined only on the basis of the desire for self-manifestation. Only when the psychological tensions in one's self are liberated and given expression does one attain the ideal of self-completeness.

In the context of Gide's plays, self-completeness implies the balance of thought and emotion, of Dionysian and Apollonian tendencies in human nature. It signifies moral and aesthetic sincerity based on the unity of the conscious and unconscious aspects in man, the fusion of sensual vitality and puritan restraint. All facets of the personality must be expressed and freed from the unconscious depths if one is to attain the integrated, harmonious ethic of Gide's Oedipus. Through the sustained intensity of debate between the satanic or diabolic and the angelic forces, one escapes the danger of static extremism in which one's personality is dominated by a single value, thought, or emotion. Because of sensual extremism, Saul—as a case in point—remains passive, and thus unable to control his spontaneous instincts. Likewise, Candaules' irrationalism betrays him. And David surrenders to the torment of his illusions. Subjected formerly to the impersonal authority of religion, Saul and David prove themselves incapable of solving their psychic disorders. Without a reasoned synthesis of conflicting values, no heroism is possible. For the Gidean hero is he who, in sustaining an inner conflict, surpasses himself and arrives at a stage of harmony which is truly—to use Nietzsche's phrase—"beyond good and evil." Such heroes are Gide's Philoctetes and Oedipus. As Gide insists: "The only drama that really interests me and that I should always be willing to depict anew is the debate of the individual with whatever keeps him from being authentic, with whatever is opposed to this integrity, to his integration." [6] For this reason, Gide's theater may be called "the theater of heroism."

[1] André Gide, *Marshlands* and *Prometheus Misbound*, tr. George D. Painter (New York, 1953), p. 54.
[2] André Gide, *My Theater*, tr. Jackson Mathews (New York, 1952), p. 272.
[3] All quotations from Gide's essay on the theater, unless otherwise indicated, are from the collection cited immediately above, *My Theater*, pp. 239-275.
[4] Cf. André Gide, *Journal*, 18 December 1905: "I want all my branches to be archer, like those the clever gardener torments to urge them to fruit."
[5] André Gide, *The Return of the Prodigal*, tr. Dorothy Bussy (London, 1953), p. 12.
[6] Gide quoted by Justin O'Brien, *Portrait of André Gide* (New York, 1953) p. 114.

II

CONSTRUCTING THE SUBJECT: *OEDIPUS*

André Gide's theater may be defined at the outset as the projection of an inner state of dialogue. To Gide a work of art is born out of spiritual conflict. Similarly, all moral reform and self-criticism discloses itself as the resolution of mental and emotional struggle. Gide's mind has justly been described as "the theater of an incessant drama." Accordingly his plays may be considered as faithful reflections of the tension between psychological extremes. They reveal and crystallize the reconciliation of intellect and desire, of the symbolic world of abstract ideas and the sensuous world of nature. In his play *Oedipus*, for example, we perceive the clash between Hebraic (Tiresias) and Hellenic (Oedipus) cultures, resulting ultimately in the affirmation of classic precision and romantic vitality of style. Such an atmosphere of conflict, to Gide, is really a sign of complete mature creativity.

As the natural medium for inner conflict, the dialogue form of the drama exemplifies Gide's approach to moral problems. By means of an analytic, psychological method, external events and outward gestures function primarily as symbolic media for projecting the emotions, thoughts, and motivations of the protagonists. In effect, the protagonists become identified with the antithetical elements of an inner dialogue. Since drama implies character, the basic experience of conflict, which is essentially moral in nature, serves as the starting point for Gide's self-searching idealism. It is also the

9

initial stage of Gide's evolution from mystical and destructive disquiet to the constructive, human, and realistic moral philosophy; from the anarchy in *Saul* and *Candaules* to the harmony of inner being in *Philoctetes* and chiefly in *Oedipus*.[1] Confronted by the moral anarchy of the times, by the "dissociation of sensibility" that afflicts modern consciousness, Gide cries out a need for a renaissance in the theater. He is primarily opposed to the naturalistic tendency of the French theater in the years preceding the first world war. In 1904 he wrote his important manifesto "The Evolution of the Theater." In it he attacked the *tranches de vue* school of Zola, the bourgeois realism of the "thesis" play. Whereas the realistic theater attempts to create an illusion of real life, discussing social and political problems of the moment, Gide lays emphasis on the purely literary qualities and on the psychological complexity of the drama. What the popular taste demands, says Gide, is the exposition of ideas that would be sympathetic to their thinking. Consequently, argument has triumphed over the poetic or evocative technique of character portrayal; thus, the actor has been stripped of his mask. In an idealistic reaction to objectivism, Gide espouses Racine's view that dramatic characters are to be appraised outside the perspective of everyday life. All attention must be focused on the spiritual drama of the hero. If the theater is to guide, not follow, popular morality, if it is to change the basic character of man, it must fashion heroic figures and present new ideals for the liberation and development of the individual. To Gide, the concept of morality is nothing else but a subjective problem.

To clarify this problem of moral self-integration, Gide proposes self-manifestation as the ideal end, and the inner dialogue of self-criticsm as the means. Catharsis is achieved when the inner conflict is externalized in dramatic form. Instead of attending to the surface phenomena as the paramount consideration, Gide concentrates on the fundamental motivations which make up the essence of the individual. Pursuing a psychological analysis of human nature, he ignores objective facts in order to penetrate more deeply to the moral conflict in the self. From this viewpoint the external vicissitudes of Saul and Candaules (in the corresponding plays) are comprehended as manifestations of an internal anarchy. In this connection, whatever ideas are supposed to be allegorized or imaged in the plays must be evaluated fundamentally as being functions of the temperament of the protagonists.

From the conflict of moral extremes, Gide moves on and arrives at order, harmony, classical balance—from the narcissistic disorder of Saul to the self-discipline of Oedipus won through self-transcendence. The moral victory of Oedipus or Philoctetes, gained through self-sacrificing experiences, proves also to be the realization of aethetic perfection. In Gide's theater, morality and aesthetics are one. And so regarding psychological insight as the basis of aesthetic complexity, Gide exploits not only the passions of love and of hate but also what, at least in his time, had never been thoroughly scrutinized: the motives of homosexuality, narcissism, and eroticism. Making his heroes the creators of their own destiny, Gide denies fate and revolts against the gods. Through the gratuitous act (*acte gratuit*), the cultivation of one's idiosyncracy, self-manifestation through self-renunciation—all significant motifs in his theater—Gide shapes his hero into being.

One of the most succinct testaments of the Gidean ethic is Gide's version of Sophocles' *Oedipus Rex*. Reinterpreting the fable, Gide transforms Oedipus the legendary hero into the role of the heroic consciousness in conflict with society, tradition, and the gods. Of course we all know how Oedipus causes his downfall by virtue of his overreaching pride, his *hubris*. Aware of the magnitude of his responsibility as king, Oedipus would not shirk the burden of avenging Laius' murder. Ironically enough his pursuit of justice proves in the end an act of self-exorcism. Besides involving parricide and incest, the play's action, in Gide's hands, becomes Oedipus' quest for his true identity.

What concerns Gide's Oedipus is not the Greek ethos but his conscience. Focused on the interior drama of Oedipus' self, the play's action revolves around Oedipus' inner dialogue. Intensely self-conscious, he asserts his presence at

11

the start: "Here I am all present and complete in this instant of everlasting time, like someone who might come down to the front of the stage and say . . . . " With Oedipus' opening gesture, Gide accomplishes two things: first, he establishes the distance between the stage and the audience by emphasizing Oedipus' actor-hood; secondly, he dispels the notion that Oedipus is simply an antiquated fiction. Oedipus himself senses his role as an actor, aware of being watched by an audience. This reflects Gide's objective attitude in his criticism of the individualist ethic portrayed in *Philoctetes*.

When Oedipus proclaims, "I felt myself to be the answer to a yet unknown question," he is echoing Gide's challenge that one must dare to be oneself. The urge to truth felt by Oedipus manifests itself in self-revelation. Believing himself a bastard gratuitously engendered in drunkenness, Oedipus prides himself on the fact that, without status or inheritance, he was able on pure merit alone to triumph over every obstacle he encountered on the way to Thebes. "Sprung from the unknown," without the past from which to draw sanction for his acts, Oedipus declares: "Everything to create, to invent, to discover. No one to resemble but myself." Consequently, his break with the past drives him to cultivate his own resources, affirming his value through painful struggle; and finally attaining conquest of himself by renouncing himself—the paradox-theme of Gide's confession *If It Die*. Like Philoctetes, Oedipus transcends human limitations in fulfilling his own heroic destiny. Urged by his relentless passion for lucid balance, he resolves to punish himself for his ignorance. In punishing himself for his egoistic "blindness" to his origin, he achieves spiritual enlightenment. Although his crime was imposed upon him (as he says) even before he was born, yet in chastizing himself he transcends his guilt. His disquiet resolved, he accepts his destiny: "I am a nameless traveller, who renounces his glory, his goods and himself."

Although a victim of tragic irony, Oedipus proves himself victorious by his self-imposed suffering, his voluntary defeat. While suffering redeems him from his crime, it also endows him with superhuman wisdom, opening up new perspectives for self-development. Consequently, he affirms that everything exists in man, that God exists within man's inner Olympus, as it were. Oedipus defines God as the totality of one's inner powers—a humanistic conception implied in the utterance: "Who would not be glad to submit to a sacred power if it leads to the position I occupy?" Further, Oedipus, inflicting retribution on himself, refuses to reconcile himself with religion. Thus, emancipated from the claims of self-interests, he contemplates the "divine obscurity." Salvation as the fulfillment of personality lies solely in Oedipus' self-denial.

From the start, Oedipus exhibits serene self-confidence. Uttering sentiments attached to his fierce individualism, he earns the censure of the Chorus which represents public opinion. The Chorus condemns him as a menace to society and religion. However, his optimism and pride is not without a certain modesty, for he recognizes that his intuitive knowledge comes from a hidden god. Needing no external restraint, free from the qualms of conscience, Oedipus is happy. To Tiresias, whose blindness seems to justify his belief in his mysteries, Oedipus' freedom from disquiet is an impiety. Because he knows no fear of God, Tiresias argues, God has punished Thebes with the plague. In the process of Socratic self-questionings, Oedipus begins to suspect his past until he discovers the truth of his origin. He thus evolves from a state of happy ignorance to that of classic wisdom. To Gide the essence of classicism lies in an "inner fidelity" to one's temperament. In sustaining this "inner fidelity," one is prepared to receive the inheritance of the past which gives unity to life. Not happiness but self-integration is Oedipus' objective.

We have now seen how Oedipus, probing into himself, reflects on god as a power which is wholly personal. Creative intuition defines Oedipus' mode of action. When he confesses, "For my part I always behave as if a god were telling me what to do," he defies the authority of organized religion, being assured of his own powers. In the spirited repartee between Oedipus and Tiresias, we observe two distinctly opposed systems of morality personified by each. While

13

Oedipus relies upon his own abilities, Tiresias considers himself an instrument of God. Whereas Oedipus stands for pure subjectivity in which chanaracter is equivalent to actions, Tiresias stands for pure objectivity which denies the free flowering of the human spirit. His authority based on the fear of God, Tiresias stands also for what is impersonal and negative: the absolutism of institutional religion, group-thinking, mystical obscurantism. Controverting Oedipus' humanism, Tiresias indicts mankind: "Every one of you is guilty before God. We cannot imagine men without stain." Opposed to the dogmatism of the priest, Oedipus' nature seeks to develop itself through inquiry and deliberation. Indeed Oedipus exemplifies the reflective, natural, progressive sage. On the other hand, Creon, in urging Oedipus to ask no questions, desires to preserve the *status quo*. He upholds the continuity of the family and the customs of society. Unlike the conservative Creon, the heir of glory by force of circumstance, Oedipus ignores his ancestry. His sole model and example is himself: "To know nothing of one's parents is a summons to excel. Toward his past Oedipus is indifferent. But the tender Jocasta is unable to accept the reality of the past and the present which she more or less apprehends; and to escape it, she commits suicide. But Oedipus demands the truth. For truth to be revealed and justice rendered, the past has to be unearthed.

What is the truth to be revealed? Nothing else but the answer to the question: "Who is Oedipus?" Oedipus himself digs the past, recalls history to memory, until finally the pattern of memory discloses the lineaments of his face. Unlike Sophocles' hero who is for modern taste a pathetic and pitiful figure, Gide's Oedipus takes the initiative to discover his guilt through independent reflection. Oedipus blinds himself not on account of self-remorse, or as a sacrifice to the divinity, but because he refuses to impute to the gods the responsibility for his crime. In other words, he would not forfeit his will and free choice by repenting before a god who after all, in making him commit a crime unknowingly, proves himself unworthy of man's tribute. And so he blinds himself, he performs a gratuitous act: self-abnegation. Declaring that "What I did I had to do, I who thought myself guided by a god," he claims all

14

responsibility, liberating himself from social conventions. Instead of being driven by his people into exile, Oedipus chooses exile. Implicitly he affirms his faith in man, not in providence, for social progress and human betterment. Opposed to the Chorus which represents subservience to political and moral systems, Oedipus becomes Gide's vehicle for a satirical critique of social institutions. At the end, Antigone vindicates Oedipus. Antigone, of course, personifies an authentic morality founded on reason and the heart. Antigone's intellectual sincerity confirms the value of Oedipus' voluntary sacrifice as witness to "the god in human good." With Gide's words we may describe Oedipus as "an example, at once grave and smiling, of what man can wrest from himself without the help of grace."[2]

The central conflict of the drama involves, therefore, the opposition between individual freedom and religious authority. Unlike Sophocles' play, which deals with the question of free will and determinism, Gide's version of the myth dwells on the issues of a personal moral crisis: in the struggle between Oedipus and Tiresias we find a semblance, an analogue, of Gide's quarrel with his Catholic friends and enemies.[3] Also, at this time in his life, Gide's imagination was moving from Dostoevsky to Marx, from the concern with particular isolated evil to the confrontation of social injustice. From this interest Gide was led to his abortive affair with communism. One must note, however, that Gide's humanistic faith derives not from ideology but from the creative individualism which, in this case, motivates Oedipus' striving for self-discovery. Believing that the gods reside deep within man, Oedipus has tried to suppress superstition and liberate man from his spiritual bondage. Accordingly, "to grow up one must look far beyond one's self." His individualism originates from the belief in the continual becoming of man, man's unceasing struggle towards self-manifestation through the exercise of self-discipline. Toward such a goal, one's intellectual awareness and spiritual energy must be directed. Admitting himself a creature of dialogue—and *Oedipus* is essentially a dialogue between the individual and the forces of conformity—Gide harnessed all the energy of his creative

15

scepticism to establish inner equilibrium in himself. Throughout his life, he was engaged with man's perennial questions concerning freedom, the nature of happiness, the mystery of desires, self-fulfillment, God.

Here in *Oedipus*, through the medium of theatrical art, Gide delivers his Promethean image of man in the person of Oedipus. By means of symbol and allegory which can be concretely apprehended, he communicates his own personal outlook, his vision of his age in this ingenious recasting of Sophocles' tragedy for his own purposes. On this point, he explains his reinterpretation of Oedipus' life as altogether different from the "grand style" of Sophocles' drama simply because he belongs to another age. In consequence, "it is to your intelligence that I address myself. I propose not to make you shudder or weep, but to make you reflect." [4] In effect, Gide wants to evoke an intellectual response to his dialectical approach toward man's enigma. Rather than appealing to any variety of primitive astonishment, he addresses the intelligence of the audience.

Such an approach is, I submit, required by the allegorical intent of most of Gide's plays. By allegory is meant loosely the projection of values into concrete symbols. Thus in this tragicomedy, Gide has created a parable of liberal rationalism overcoming romantic mysticism, self-indulgence being cast out for an optimistic and progressive humanism which treats evil as an inhuman fiction that should be surpassed. Instead of adopting the pre-Socratic "pity and terror formula" with its somber primitive overtones, Gide adopts a philosophical, dialectic method. Such a method epitomizes the inner dialogue of the self. Also it approximates the clash between Oedipus and Tiresias. In his struggle, Oedipus exemplifies the instincts of order and design controlling physical violence, subordinating disasters of family history through a spiritual synthesis. On the whole, Oedipus incarnates Gide's revolt against the dehumanizing forces of his time, his belief in man's perpetual realization of his possible selves. *Oedipus* presents man's ordeal in the labyrinth of himself as a step toward self-integration.

Unlike Sophocles, Gide introduces Oedipus' children into the central situation of the play. Precocious and gifted with acute percipience, Eteocles and Polynices suggest the French youth after the first world war with all their confused amoralism and romantic cynicism. Here Gide uses them to speak out his own thoughts.[5] Learning (through the device of eavesdropping) Eteocles' wish to sleep with his sister Ismene, Oedipus scolds his son. Eteocles and Polynices are both looking for an authorization, an "honorable motive" for incest, a deed of which they are the very fruits. Not only are the two boys well acquainted with Freud's theories—an ironic anachronism—but they are also cognizant of the *mal du siecle*, the subject of Eteocle's treatise. To Eteocles, the malady of the age lies in man's endless self-questioning which has grown intense until it paralyzes sensibility (as in *Saul*) and renders one impotent to act.

Of their attitudes Oedipus comments: "Of my example they have only taken what flatters them, authorizations and licence, letting pass constraint, the difficult and the better." Implicitly he condemns his effete disciples for their misinterpretations of his ethics. While the two boys mirror in their moods the perplexities of awakening consciousness, they also signify the continuity of the family. To them Oedipus hands the legacy of his life's lesson: self-discipline. Further, he exhorts them to contemplate the phenomenon of man as the first word of wisdom. In the two sisters we find examples of antithetical movements. Unlike her sister Ismene—sensitive, naive, the embodiment of self-seeking joy—Antigone, the daughter of sorrow, personifies charity and intense faith. Not only does she want to nurse the victims of the plague, but also she wants to intercede for her father's sins, finding love for him rather than for God a more self-fulfilling task. To Antigone, virtue is only a reflection of God who is its fountainhead. Earlier, when she utters, "the more I love him, the more I fear the happiness of which he boasts," she anticipates Oedipus' fall. With the sincerity of her worship, she reinforces the redeeming value of Oedipus' self-expiation.

One will observe how Gide, in using bare, direct colloquial prose, aims to connect the archaic material he exploits with modern idiom. Although there is a certain objective stylization in the speeches of Oedipus, humorous overtones are not lacking throughout. For example, the Chorus, unaware of their incongruity, narrate how they killed and stewed the sacred birds of augury to stave off their hunger. This quality of humor, almost a discordant facetiousness, is present also in the genteel Creon's reaction to Oedipus' crime: "Not to know if he's my brother-in-law or my nephew!" (Incidentally, Gide's chorus does not possess the traditional decorum which characterizes the Greek tragic chorus.) On the whole, the use of humor serves to heighten by contrast the tragic irony of the play, providing also a counterpoise to the intellectualized interplay of attitudes.

Together with parodies of the old legend and its allusions to contemporary facts, Gide creates in this tragicomedy an illusion of modernity in keeping with his intention of diagnosing the malady of his age through a subtle retouching of ancient text. As proof of the organic unity and coherence of the play, we can isolate Gide's preparations for future developments in the early stages of the play. In Act I, for example, Oedipus already provides a clue to the resolution when he exclaims: "Jocasta has always watched over my happiness. She is perfect, Jocasta, what a wife! And what a mother! For me, who never knew my own mother, she has been a wife and mother in one." Such a jocular statement sharply witnesses to the tragic irony of Oedipus' fate. Besides forecasting the ultimate solution in an unknowing way, Creon's advice to Oedipus epitomizes the whole evolution of Oedipus' life: "Whoever killed him did it for you; he played your game; it's not for you to punish him, but reward him." Speaking of the murder, Oedipus anticipates the play's denouement: "He'll not escape me—that I swear—." And how true indeed! With Oedipus' discipline to "Be simply yourself: direct as an arrow—straight to the target—" coincides with the classic directness and simplicity of the play's movement. One perceives further how Gide avoids elaborate expositions, idiosyncratic characters, and secondary plots to reinforce the structural unity of the play.

¹ See André Gide, *My Theater*, tr. Jackson Mathews (New York, 1952); *Two Legends*, tr. John Russell (New York, 1950).

² Gide quoted by John Russell, p. ix.

³ See Justin O'Brien, *Portrait of André Gide: A Critical Biography* (New York, 1953), pp. 227ff.

⁴ Quoted by Van Meter Ames, *André Gide* (New York, 1947), p. 115.

⁵ In his book *André Gide* (New York, 1951), p. 160, George D. Painter suggests that: "there is an allegory of the early death of Gide's father, of Gide's half-incestuous marriage immediately after he had lost his mother, with his cousin her substitute."

III

DIALECTIC OF MASKS: PHILOCTETES: THE TREATISE ON THREE ETHICS

The understanding of Gide's play *Philoctetes*[1] largely depends on our perception of its underlying dialectic of masks. This dialectical process is the dramatic agency employed by Gide in order to define the human condition by symbolic indirection. The three protagonists form a triangle of tensions, of conflicting interests from which the psychological conflict evolves. It may appear at first glance that the characters are too idealized, too perfectly cut out for each of them to represent a definite value or a fixed idea. But this obtrusive quality of the parable seems precisely to be the effect pursued: through the allegorical status of the characters, Gide establishes an atmosphere of remoteness from actuality. Insofar as abstract ideals are mirrored in the moods and decisions of the characters, the drama is engaged with the projection of these clashing ideals. With the unfolding of each personality, the structure of the plot reveals itself; the modes of implied oppositions become explicit. Expectation is generated, followed by fulfillment, in the evolution of various motives.

At the outset, we are then confronted with the play's literal problem, namely, how Ulysses can conquer Philoctetes' antipathy, and then dispossess him of Hercules' bow, the bow being the main object of the hunt. Factually stated, this simple scheme is the plot. But of course more significance inheres in the process than in the mere outcome of this scheme. Act I presents a unique setting: "A level waste of snow and ice; a low gray sky"[2] Snow and ice imply rigor, discipline, single-mindedness. The whole landscape suggests a Platonic paradise of eternal Forms. Instead of passions, love, dream, or illusion, here is a world of pure thought and abstraction, a place where everything is free from the flux of time and becoming. Everything manifests itself in gesture, everything is transparent and endowed with a permanent crystalline beauty. In this clarity of solitude, thought and action, motive and deed merge and are one. Such geographical frigidity mirrors the loneliness of pure being, the tranquility of Philoctetes' mind. Neoptolemus interprets the scene thus: "This seems like death already, here; every hour my mind has been growing so much colder, and purer, all passion gone, that now nothing is left but for the body to die."[3] This setting foreshadows Philoctetes' sublime self-abnegation, his total self-surrender at the end.

When Neoptolemus expresses his desire to be sacrificed to the gods, he recalls the case of Philoctetes whose fortunes, up to the opening play, are summarized in retrospect by Ulysses. While Neoptolemus, in his first speech, describes the background voyage and reports the stalemate of the Trojan war, Ulysses recalls the onset of the war itself. He recounts the hardships encountered by the Greeks on their journey, culminating finally in the peculiar accident that befell Philoctetes. Volunteering to be sacrificed, Philoctetes finds himself bitten by a snake: chance foils his will. For the snake-bite, causing him to wail and cry agonizingly, reduces him to a pitiable object. He is then ostracized as a dispiriting element. Thus one cannot volunteer to be sacrificed; rather, one is chosen. The accident of destiny selects Philoctetes to be sacrificed, in a sense, by being cast out of the community of warriors. Like a corpse, he is then abandoned on a wintry island. As befits a warrior's body, he is left his bow and arrows, the object of Ulysses' mission. According to Ulysses, Philoctetes has been sacrificed to save the army's courage, thus preventing a case which would "subject the courage of a whole army . . . to the suffering and wailing of a single man."[4]

22

Rightly enough he justifies himself in the name of the gods exalted by the Greek city-state. While Ulysses recollects the past in order to foresee the reality of the future, Neoptolemus is bound to the present, utterly obsessed with his own welfare.

One will observe that Ulysses defends the exile of Philoctetes on the basis of human frailty. Philoctetes' obsession with the pain of his world and his physical agony is a "human-all-too-human" fault, which cannot be allowed to arouse pity and thus demoralize the Greek army. Pity is exorcised; indulgence on bodily afflictions cannot be countenanced; and devotion to Greece is the supreme meaning of existence. Ulysses proclaims: "all passion put behind us, our great destinies at last are to be resolved, and our hearts, here, more completely dedicated, are at last to achieve the most perfect virtue." [5] "Perfect virtue" here may be defined as self-immolation to the gods of the Greek city-state. In spite of his passionless bearing, Ulysses is not depicted as a flat, one-dimensional character. His determined air, we discover, comes out of restraint and utmost self-control. Like Neoptolemus, who objects to betraying his father's friend, Ulysses himself would censure his crafty designs against his friend. But Ulysses is prodded on: "The god's commands are cruel; they are the gods."[6] Thus Ulysses convinces Neoptolemus, son of Achilles, to ignore his father's precept and help him fulfill his mission. The country far surpasses the virtue of comradeship—an argument confirmed by Achilles' service itself. In this crisis of loyalties, virtue becomes, for Ulysses, an exaltation of duty to the city-state. Life, friendship, even Neoptolemus' innocence—all are offered to the country's cause. Denying his will, Ulysses throws all responsibility to the gods of the country.

By the end of Act I, the exchange between Ulysses and Neoptolemus, which prepares the stage for the entrance of Philoctetes, is interrupted by the singing of Philoctetes. At this point, Neoptolemus assumes the role of narrator and relates to the audience Philoctetes' outrageous complaints. Upon sensing the presence of strangers, Philoctetes grows silent, belying Ulysses' prediction. Doubtless time has wrought changes on Philoctetes' soul. Act II concerns itself with

23

exhibiting his new personality. To this exile, virtue is shown by "a pure and truly disinterested action,"[7] whereby all pure radiance and beauty of conduct assumes an aesthetic finality. Thus: "To whom would I need to appear what I am? My only care is to be."[8] The social conformist will never attain virtue in this sense, for it is the fruit of self-communion, beyond the distractions of pity, pain, or any interest. Instead of simply *being*, the conformist strives to *appear*, to put on an appearance.

Opposing his beliefs to that of Philoctetes, Ulysses gives credit to Philoctetes for having ceased to hate the Greeks. Assured that he has become less Greek and more man, Philoctetes succumbs to weeping on hearing of Achilles' death—a proof that he has not ceased to be a blood-and -flesh creature.[9] Like Narcissus, he has discovered his essence in loneliness. He now expresses himself better in giving utterance to nature's distress, annihilating himself in the rapturous articulation of nature's barrenness. We perceive here the spectacle of Philoctetes in the act of shifting from the socio-ethical stage to the aesthetic realm, from the Dionysian ecstasy to the serene Apollonian vision. The transformation of Philoctetes exemplifies Gide's creed discerned in a miraculous paradox, namely, that "through renunciation every virtue finds fulfillment." [10]

The detachment of Philoctetes springs from his fated isolation, his estrangement from society and its conventions. To Gide, the source of all hypocrisy is society and its artificial compromises. Holding up, as it were, the mirror to nature, Philoctetes meditates on the purity that is born out of articulating the sufferings of the world around him. To all these gestures, Ulysses displays an amused attitude. To be sure, Philoctetes' identity is now definable only in terms of one or several of his acts. Freed from the dominion of time he has become eternal: "nothing becomes . . . everything is, everything remains."[11] Now his actions, by means of which he reveals himself, seem to have been embodied in rocks and ice, literally petrified, and thus have become rigid and abstract though beautiful emblems of permanence. Here prevails an absolute unity and correspondence between intent and

24

gesture, being and becoming, essence and existence. In the stasis of his surroundings, Philoctetes has acquired a new awareness: "all my passion is quieted, and I feel the Truth always firmer—and I should wish my actions likewise always sounder and more beautiful . . . I do not wish to stop a single ray of Zeus; let him transpierce me, Ulysses, like a prism, and the refracted light make my acts loveable and beautiful."[12] That prism-image certainly alludes to Gide's idea of man's inexhaustible possibilities and their fulfillment through every form of action, making the self finally transparent. This dominant metaphor of crystal, with the purity of its hard cold surface, connotes also the ideal of absolute sincerity in art as well as in life.

In Act III, we behold Philoctetes announcing his discovery of Ulysses' strategy to deceive him. His confidence has almost been won by the boy's interest in him when he fortuitously overhears the dialogue between Ulysses and Neoptolemus. Neoptolemus is being used as a bait, and his innocence exploited. Through cunning and deceit Ulysses would impose his virtue on Philoctetes. Out of remorseful pity, however, Neoptolemus sides with Philoctetes and betrays Ulysses. No doubt Neoptolemus represents that stage of youthful indecisiveness in which one has as yet no fixed beliefs and when the mind is still flexible. Coming into contact with Ulysses, the unsuspecting Philoctetes loses his detachment for a while: he is thrown back to the demands of his ego. Hoping much from the friendship offered by the two Greeks, Philoctetes becomes self-conscious. But soon he recoils, surprised and disillusioned, from the impact of discovering Ulysses' duplicity. Virtue truly blossoms alone where human interests are non-existent. Although he suspects the feigned earnestness of Neoptolemus, Philoctetes acts with sheer self-confident spontaneity toward him. At this point he tries to formulate in words his conception of virtue as an allegiance to something higher than the gods—but he fails, for the intellect cannot comprehend an aesthetic experience. Philoctetes can only dramatize virtue, transmuting his self-devotion in the visible spectacle of relinquishing voluntarily his life-sustaining bow.

25

Meanwhile the patriot Ulysses persists in his notion of virtue as devotion to the state. Such a notion of virtue is founded on the devotion to the collective welfare which sanctions the abrogation of individual rights for the sake of the majority. Actually, such a devotion is selfish because in the end one acquires a sense of superiority over others. On this pride of appearance rests the structure of the state, the collective self-interest. Since they are merely projections of Greek aspirations, the gods are nothing else but nationalist partisans. To something else beyond the gods, namely, to oneself, Philoctetes would devote himself. And so he aspires for a total self-surrender. Virtue, to him, is what "one undertakes beyond one's strength." To achieve self-transcendence, he must of necessity suffer the pain of freely yielding his bow, symbolic of his pride, in order to gain self-transparency or the fullness of identity. His solitary quest for virtue culminates in the performance of an aesthetic gratuitous act. By pretending thatNeoptolenus has succeeded in administering the drug to induce unconsciousness, Philoctetes makes Ulysses believe that his craftiness has triumphed.

In truth, however, Philoctetes' self-denial triumphs over the limited knowledge of Ulysses. Admiring Philoctetes' self-denial, Ulysses himself admits his defeat. In this light, self-transparency consists in absolute disinterestedness, aesthetic detachment, or "denudation." We have stated how, in his solitude, Philoctetes' cries of pain have become disinterested and beautiful for lack of any human listener. Transferred to suffering nature, his afflictions assume an objectivity which the artist can contemplate with detachment. Indeed, Philoctetes has become an artist; ethics metamorphoses into aesthetics.[13] Only when words and actions bear no ulterior motive, when conduct is purified of egoism, do they take on the form of beauty; and creative beauty, not goodness, seems to be the ideal of such a morality shown by Philoctetes. Art of course is totally disinterested and knows no utilitarian end. Beauty is alien to society since society is at bottom a network of personal interests. Abandoning his attachment to the world by yielding his bow, his link with the Greek community,

Philoctetes surpasses his limited ego and emerges to a realm of absolute freedom. As a whole, the play is remarkable for its unrelenting development. With its spare, chastened idiom, the circular action has classic directness and simplicity. The play reaches its crisis when Philoctetes accepts the sacrifice of his possession, acquiring again the profound peace he used to enjoy before Ulysses' arrival. Unlike Sophocles, Gide assigns the resolution of the conflict between Ulysses and Philoctetes to the latter's voluntary acquiescence: his self-renunciation. Instead of using a *deus ex machina*, aided with force and cunning, to compel Philoctetes' submission, Gide makes his protagonist a Promethean hero: his self-transcendence becomes the proof of an inner fidelity to his essence. Such self-assertion overshadows the value of life itself; hence, Philoctetes gives up his bow, his only means of survival.[14] With the loss of Philoctetes' consciousness, signifying the death of the self, and his awakening, there is an allusion to the archetypal pattern of major myths, involving the death and resurrection of a Dionysian god. Finally, there prevails an almost beatific harmony when even nature seems to affirm the happiness of Philoctetes in his self-sufficiency. Such a heroic beatitude is reflected by the stage directions: "His voice has become extraordinarily mild and beautiful; around him flowers are showing through the snow, and birds from heaven come down to feed him."[15]

Insofar as Gide has pursued consistently the logic between cause and effect, idea and image, the play achieves its allegorical intent through a dialectic of self-projections. But what really counts in this dramatized discourse, this philosophical dialogue, are precisely those epiphanic gestures which reveal an internal coherence between motive and deed, whereby we suspend disbelief and accept the drama as significant poetic configuration.[16] We witness Ulysses' mode of representing the idea of social conformity; Neoptolemus, of youthful innocence and self-indulgence; Philoctetes, of the concept of virtue as gratuitous action. In this play Gide then reinterprets the legend of Philoctetes as a drama of personal conscience, of a search for being and identity. Born out of a dialectic between masks of psychological polarities, such a conscience affirms its ethic through a memorable paradox—a central idea in all of Gide's plays: "Except a grain of wheat fall into the earth and die, it abideth by itself alone; but if it die, it beareth much fruit."[17]

[1] All quotations from Philoctetes are from André Gide, My Theater, tr. Jackson Mathews (New York, 1952). For the play's biographical context, see Jean Delay, The Youth of André Gide, tr. J. Guicharnand (Chicago, 1963), pp. 366-367; also, André Gide-Paul Valery, Correspondence (Librarie Gallimard, 1955), pp. 346-349; James Clark MacLaren, The Theatre of André Gide (Baltimore, 1953), pp. 20-25.

[2] Ibid., p. 145.

[3] Ibid.,p. 147.

[4] Ibid., p.149.

[5] I bid., p. 150.

[6] Ibid., p. 151.

[7] Ibid., p. 158.

[8] Ibid.

[9] See Justin O'Brien, Portrait of André Gide: A Critical Biography (New York, 1953), p. 145; also Albert J. Guerard, André Gide (Cambridge, England, 1953), pp. 24-28.

[10] Quoted by O'Brien, p. 310. Cf. Jean Pierre Beujot, "Du bon usage de l'amour de soi," Prétexte (Paris, 1952), pp. 51-53.

[11] Le Théâtre, p. 163.

[12] Ibid.

[13] Cf. Laurence Thomas, André Gide: The Ethic of the Artist (London, 1950), p. 106; also Günther Krebber Untersuchungen zur Aesthetik und Kritik André Gides(Genève, 1959), pp. 15ff.; Gerd Lansfuss, DerÄsthetizismus André Gides in der Ästhetischen Bildung (Münster, Westphalen, 1959), pp. 217-367.

[14] See Elsie Pell, André Gide: l'évolution de sa pensée religieuse (Grenoble, 1935), pp. 71-114; Leon Pierre-Quint, André Gide (Paris, 1933), pp. 73-159; R. M. Aberes, L'Odyssée d'André Gide (Paris, 1953), pp. 129-144.

[15] Le Theatre, p. 180.

[16] Cf Marc Beigbeder, André Gide (Paris, 1954), pp. 67-94; Helmut Uhlig, André Gide (Berlin, 1948), pp. 32ff.; Lotte SchreiberLeben und Denken im Werk von André Gide (Berlin, 1933), pp. 19-33; Goran Schildt, Gide et l'homme (Paris, 1929), pp. 30-64.

[17] The Journals of André Gide, ed. Justin O'Brien (New York, 1951), Vol. I, p. 351.

IV

SAUL
THE TEMPTATION OF WILLING
ONE'S FATE

In the predicament of Saul we perceive how the diabolic force of narcissism destroys the balance of the inner dialogue of the self.[1] This inner dialogue of the self dictates in essence the pattern and significance of all Gide's plays. In effect Saul's will, possessed and overcome by the demons of his instincts, decays until he suffers a moral collapse. Because he retreats into a world of dreams and illusion so that he inhibits the exercise of his own will, he is unable to integrate himself with reality.

At the start Saul finds himself forsaken by God and besieged by his enemies. Waiting for the future to reveal itself, he plunges into a state of introversion and inaction. In time he finds himself dominated by his sensual, satanic urges. His love for David, his sexual inversion, drives him to kill his wife in a fit of jealousy. His wife dead, Saul yields the more readily to his abnormal passion. This inverted affection in turn causes his passivity and prevents him from confronting actively the reality of his situation. With his "welcoming disposition" as his idiosyncrasy, Saul indulges his vices. The demons that taunt and cajole him are nothing else but incarnations of his ignoble passion: the temptations of the senses. They emanate from his exuberant personality, his "hypersensibility," which endows him with keen powers of

29

sensuous perception. His senses solicited by nature, Saul's will deteriorates. In the end his sensitive temperament betrays him. From his diseased will arises his tragic fall. Instead of attending to his moral and political responsibility, he cultivates his temperament which, to him, is more important than his soul's salvation. Thus his failure to control his instincts leads to his demoralization, defeat, and death. Essentially he has failed to balance his hedonism, his satanic ethics, with the restraints afforded by the rational intellect.

Gide seems to be offering here a counterpoise and antidote to the extreme sensualist philosophy of his preceding work *Les Nourritures terrestres (The Fruits of the Earth)*. Concentrating on the psychological dialogue in Saul's consciousness, Gide shows the moral degeneration of an undisciplined nature when conscience and intellect are ousted by the glorification of the senses. Saul's complicated personality reflects the conflict between the mind and the body, the Dionysian and Apollonian tendencies in the self. Instead of struggling against the Dionysian force in himself, Saul elects, in the crisis, the torments of sensual possession. His only consolation lies in gratifying his own desires. He protects his desires, becoming in the process pitifully passive and apathetic to the forces that aim to destroy him. Because he values his anarchic temperament more than his kinghood, he makes no effort to maintain leadership among men. Virtually enslaved by his desires, his will disintegrates; he then acts spasmodically, by turns cruel and tender, self-pitying and perverse, till he is reduced to a Lear-like imbecility. What disturbs the inner dialogue of the self here is the hubris of his sensuality, thus suppressing the organic growth of personality. Unable to externalize the tensions within himself, he becomes blind to the moral issues before him. We see now his act of discarding his beard to look aged and austere to David proves his escapism: Saul then succumbs to inertia. In effect David's conquest of Saul symbolizes the triumph of Saul's desires over his life. A fugitive from moral conflict, Saul brings about the annihilation of his personality by a non-resistance to temptation.

In the last act, Gide reveals the tragic self-awareness of his main character. On the eve of his downfall Saul cries out: "My value lies in my complexity." Indeed Saul is a complex personality who bears a striking resemblance to Lear. In fact, Gide has Shakespeare's play in mind when he began writing *Saul*.[2] But here the daughters of Lear are completely embodied in the comic, fanciful demons who figure in the opening scenes. Each of these demons personifies one of Saul's passions: fury or madness, lust, fear, doubt, power, and vanity. We see the demon of vanity merging with his purple robe, Legion sitting on his crown. With his human failings objectified, Gide foreshadows the struggles of Saul. Precisely these passions serve as the motivations of his decisions and actions. To be sure, Saul's enemy lies within himself. His tragic fault stems from his urge to yield to his sensual inclinations. However, instead of renouncing responsibility, Saul manifests a tragic acceptance of his lot, crying out defiantly: "What shall console a man for his degradation, if not that which degraded him?"

Through the talk of the demons at the opening of the play, we are introduced to the situation of Saul. Disturbed by the Philistine's threat to his power, he seeks knowledge of the future. Reading the stars, he discovers that his son Jonathan will not succeed him to the throne, that his dynasty will end. In order to ensure this premonition as his own secret, he orders the execution of all sorcerers. Meanwhile his anguished self burns in his nervous sensitivity: "The slightest noise, the slightest fragrance, takes my attention: my senses are turned outward, and no sweetness passes me unperceived." With all the sorcerers killed, the demons of the passions who plague only the future flock to Saul's throne. We have remarked already that the demons function as concrete projections of Saul's sensual excesses. With this device Saul's infirmities are rendered objectively visible with a certain degree of plausibility and dramatic particularity. Further, in their comic exchanges, the past is revealed and the stage set for Saul's entrance.

Is Saul's fate pre-ordained? It is not difficult to see how Saul, with some element of *amor fati*, wills his destruction

31

when, in the last act, he refuses to escape. One conceives of Saul's freedom then as proved by his willed self-indulgence. In his fidelity to his temptations, Saul refuses to save himself from immanent destruction. Like his fault of extreme sensuality, his introspectiveness paralyzes his will-power: "Ah, what am I waiting for now? Why do I not get up and act? My will! My will! I call to it now like a shipwrecked sailor hailing a ship he sees disappearing in the distance—going, going . . . . I strengthen everything against me." Certainly the attenuation of his self-control derives from the surfeit of all his desires. When he wants to pray, the demon taunts him: "Don't tell me it wasn't for your pleasure that you brought me in—eh? to have me in the fold of your cloak?" On the eve of his death, Saul welcomes all his demons: "Come in! If I refused my lodging to a single one, I should be afraid it might be the most attractive—or maybe the most wretched." To paraphrase his speech: If I suppress my impulses from exercising their powers over me, I feel that they might revenge themselves upon me in more insidious if not compulsive ways.[3] Apprehending his coming death, oppressed by his demons, he justifies himself: "Shall I find any remedy for my desire other than its satisfaction?"

Admitting certain qualifications, Saul may be considered one of Gide's exemplary heroes. Routed by his human failings, Saul could not accept all the consequences of his ambiguous actions. In nourishing his desires to absurdity, he liberates himself from their bondage precisely by gratifying them. However, when practised by a king, this virtue of fulfilling one's needs tends to jeopardize the duties which a king is supposed to attend to. Saul courts disaster in looking only after his own personal concerns, ignoring his social responsibility. By virtue of his mortal defects, Saul assumes a representative role. Moreover, his unpredictability, his gratuitous actions, redeem him from the curse of the average and the ordinary. At one point Saul stabs the queen without any definite motive. Of Saul's malady the queen says: " . . . his will has overreached itself and needs to be directed." Saul's enigma becomes more clarified by the dying words of the

Witch of Endor: "All that delights you is your enemy . . . . Free yourself!"

The theme of homosexuality is played out in Saul's fascination for David, his enemy. Earlier, the Witch of Endor pointed out this fatal obsession of Saul. With this inverted affection for David, Saul relinquishes all concern with his kingdom's affairs. This love of his enemy constitutes the dreadful secret that makes Saul's crown heavy. But actually Saul's foe is not David nor any visible force outside; rather, his enemy is the compelling and fatal nature of his desires. Had not the queen condemned Saul with her dying words "Henceforth be dangerous to yourself"? In the last act, Saul admits that he has been "a man of desires." Heedless of the demons' cajoling, he remonstrates: "My God, what am I before thee"—and in the pause the demons cry out his name to stress his personal responsability—"that thou shouldst overwhelm me with desire?" Immediately another image fits in to distract his meditation: "What I love in him, above all, is his strength. The movement of his loins is beautiful!" David looms once more as his nemesis. In thus desiring David, Saul desires his own ruin. Saul's homosexual attitude reveals itself when, hearing David and Jonathan converse, he cries out: "Oh, tortures! Mortification of the flesh!" Seeing David clothed with all the insignia of royalty, he exclaims: "I am suffering martyrdom . . . . " Although he despises his son Jonathan for being womanish, yet Saul willingly identifies himself with Jonathan who is loved by David.

In the crucial encounter with the Witch of Endor, Saul's motivations are finally laid bare. Foreshadowing the play's denouement, the Ghost of Samuel probes into Saul's inner condition, his "unspeakable torment" of the soul: "You know very well that what you call fear is really desire . . . You have taken the enemy to your heart . . . . " According to Samuel, Saul's error lies in his having received David, in harboring love for his enemy. Although he excuses this error by saying that God has chosen David, Saul hears Samuel's censure: "Do you think that God did not foresee long ago the final faltering of your soul and decide to punish you?" When Samuel prophesies the defeat of Saul, Saul loses consciousness. Being left ignorant of the future, Saul could still will his actions freely and thus admit full responsibility for their results. Nevertheless, Saul surrenders himself to his perverse passion for David in spite of his knowledge that "all deliciousness is hostile." With full awareness Saul enacts his own fate: "Am I henceforth to grope alone forever in the dark?"

In the last act, Joel observes that "Saul's defeat is already accomplished in his heart." Saul confesses this defeat implicitly: "I haven't the strength within me. It is true . . . I should come nearer to God." We have remarked earlier on Saul's need to repent in the mock-trial with the priest. Saul exhorts the priest in that scene to accuse, question, and judge him—but that is all done flippantly. His need to justify himself sounds serious at first, but the tone of earnestness subsides later to mere petulance. Troubled by his inability to make decisions, he defends himself: "There are more important affairs than those of the kingdom—and they concern no one but me . . . . "Joel is the person who, earlier, correctly diagnosed the gratuitous nature of Saul's acts: "His decisions seem to have no motive." Joel, of course, is the man of political calculation; hence, he switches loyalty and kills his former master Saul traitorously. The Barber, on the other hand, exemplifies the flat character who finds self-fulfillment in submission to a master; "One's interests are rather complex. Whom is one to serve? All I ask is to devote myself." Ultimately, however, both the Barber and Saul are answering, each in his own way, the question: "Who am I?" The two comic figures of the Barber and Joel, in discussing Saul's psychological state, furnish examples of indirect portrayal of character.[4] Because they belong to the sphere of normality, their comments counterbalance the self-justification of Saul. Their viewpoint represents the common and ordinary man. At this point, we may note also certain comic passages that relieve the gravity of Saul's "satanic" exploits. When Saul (in Act IV), defiant at his disobedient subjects, hurls his javelin clumsily, the spectacle he presents is funny and ridiculous. When Saul sneezes, the Demon quips "Bless you." Joel also parodies Saul in describing him the "King of Sweepers" because he can "sweep" away the lives of any man. In providing a comic counterpoise to Saul's despair, the impish demons and their banter sound as a recurrent motif in the texture of the play. And in the mock-trial between the priest and Saul, we find also the humorous strains balancing the somber chords of Saul's anguish.

Pursuing the principle of dramatic distance, Gide shatters the continuity of the play's action by making Saul (in Act V, scene 2) come forward to the footlights to address the audience: "With what shall man console himself for a fall if not with what made him fall?" The illusion of reality is therefore dispelled precisely in accord with Gide's concept of theatrical detachment as proposed in his essay "The Evolution of the Theater."[5] Besides expressing the heroic self-consciousness of Saul, his speech harks back to the beginning of his downfall. On the eve of his death Saul imparts to us the lucid vision of his life as a search for identity. In *Saul*, as well as in *Philoctetes* and *Candaules*, Gide is concerned with the rule: "Dare to be yourself."[6]

---

[1] The text of Saul is in André Gide, *My Theater*, tr. Jackson Mathews (New York, 1952), pp. 1-17.

[2] Witnessed by Gide's letter: "I shall write a poem in which I shall compare my desires to the daughters of King Lear, for I feel like unto the dispossessed king for having listened to the passions that charm me." Quoted by Justin O'Brien, *Portrait of André Gide: A Critical Biography* (New York, 1953), p. 165.

[3] On one occasion Gide confessed: "Some people work over themselves to obtain the unity of their person. I let myself go," quoted by O'Brien, p. 167.

[4] Another traditional convention Gide uses is the aside, thus giving us a glimpse into the secret workings of the protagonist's mind.

[5] See Gide's important essay on the theater, "The Evolution of the Theater," *My Theater*, pp. 259-275. This is a lecture delivered at the *Société de la Libre Esthétique*, Brussels, March 25, 1904.

[6] Quoted by O'Brien, p. 168.

V

KING CANDAULES:
EROS UNBOUND—
TOWARD SELF-TRANSCENDENCE

"Every new gift that comes to us brings with it a new desire to test it out. To possess is to experiment," declares King Candaules at the beginning of the play. To experiment, to plunge into an abyss of uncalculated risks—such is the ambition of this noble and generous soul. Through an act of limitless generosity, Candaules transcends himself in manifesting what lies within him, what is given in his nature. To Gide, heroism lies in the supreme duty of being sincere to oneself, of *being* instead of simply *appearing*. One is awed indeed by the logical ruthlessness with which Candaules translates his wanton thought into practice. Thus, his excessive kindness corrupts innocence itself in the person of Gyges, and exposes him to death. Although his life is now saturated with happiness, he believes that his happiness is incomplete unless he shares it with others. He would not want to enjoy anything in secret: others must share, for instance, the joy of contemplating his wife's beauty. While the poor man consumes himself to gain what he desires, the rich man risks what he possesses. The risk, this daring gamble, is Candaules' prime motivation in the play.[1]

In Act I we learn how, in order to measure the depth of his happiness, Candaules has been holding exuberant feasts for some time. Flatterers and hypocrites, the counterpart of

Saul's demons, gather around him. Esteeming the banquet more than the banquet-giver, Sephax, for instance, concentrates on indulging himself in food and drink. Likewise, Pharnaces extols the king for satisfying his appetite. But Syphax, on the other hand, feels that Candaules is motivated not by a positive virtue but some "vague generosity." On the whole, each of the courtiers bears a malicious opinion of Candaules' intent. Consequently, their opinions of the king are simply what they observe of his appearance. Not to discriminate between what is false and what is sincere—that is, argues Nicomedes, the key to happiness. In contrast with their fawning habits, Gyges the fisherman vows that he will never deceive the king. Indeed, the king's happiness is too overwhelming for him to partake of. With naive simplicity, the humble Gyges says that it is better to have little so that, unlike the king's wealth, one can possess it solely and completely. But to Candaules, happiness "exists only in the knowledge that others have of it"; alone by himself, his bounty and the voluptuous beauty of the queen truly escape him.

To Gyges, who has only few possessions of value, happiness is easily grasped. But soon an accident committed by his wife leads to the destruction of his cabin and nets. Then on discovering his wife's infidelity, Gyges stabs her. By this act of revenge he affirms the queen's conviction that happiness is killed in sharing. The queen judges Gyges' deed: "He was right to kill her. Belonging to two—oh, it's horrible!" Left alone with his poverty, his sole happiness, Gyges even loses this happiness with Candaules' gifts. In spite of the king's favors, he grieves, wholly disappointed and dispossessed. When Gyges, in killing his wife, renounces his only joy, Candaules considers him his noble friend. At this point, the flatterers begin to sense the dangerous nature of Candaules' joy. When he displays the queen's unveiled face to the crowd, he justifies his act: "To be alone in the enjoyment of her has made me suffer much." Indeed his happiness depends wholly on that of others: " . . . that I truly possess only when others know that I possess." For this reason he prods Gyges to possess Nyssia the queen. Understandably enough, as he succumbs to Gyges' knife-blow, he utters: "I felt nothing in me but kindness." We remark too that after Gyges' violation of the queen, Candaules sobers up for a while. Once more he feels the urge of keeping Nyssia selfishly, for himself alone. But it is too late; for Nyssia, outraged by the deception, vigorously exhorts Gyges: "Yes, and he was my husband! Kill him! He betrayed me." To her, happiness is destroyed when shared. The queen's fury over her betrayal resembles Gyges' vindictive rage against his wife's infidelity. There is one striking transformation here: while Gyges' first killing reduces him to utmost poverty, this last elevates him to kinghood.

What makes Candaules an exceptional character, I submit, is his inscrutable inclination towards the non-moral, the absurd. His temperament leads him to dare the perils of an unknown path of action. When he ventures to share his wife with Gyges, he attempts to determine the limits of his magnanimity. It seems that, in this context, death is the only frontier for this pioneer into the absurd realms of a man's possibilities. To find out what man can realize of himself, the utmost courage he can summon out of himself—such is the arduous task of the heroic will. What is rendered here in dramatic sequence is the tragic commitment of Candaules to the heroic task of being what he is; in short, of self-fulfillment. But what is the real core of Candaules' unrest? One commentator elucidates this crux:

> ...the "Communism" of this exquisite Pandarus is not a function of intellect and will but of that sheer sensibility whose acute perception of essence connotes a luxurious obliviousness to moral order. And the denial of hierarchy, the abdication—in every sense—of the more-and-less than human king, is a projection into art, not only of an aesthete's vision of life, but of the implications of Gide's personal situation—those implications which the noble "hypocrisy" of art, he himself insists, permits him to indicate. This play of indulgence is itself the indulgence of a "possibility"—a possibility of the erotic imagination with its endless capacity for deflecting the natural.[2]

In this play, Gide concerns himself largely with the "epiphany" of the heroic character. His main interest is the dramatic rendition of Candaules' strange psychology. Other personages, background, and incident are important only insofar as they contribute to the credibility of his actions, the unfolding of the hero's nature. Candaules appears here as the victim of a volatile sensibility. While he is exceedingly aware of moral values, he defies the existing moral order and ignores traditional restraints. His sensibility, led by an irresistible urge to be "generous to the point of vice," drives him to extremes. From the "vice of generosity" Candaules derives his only pleasure. Indulging the blind, dark instincts of his nature, Candaules deprives himself of concentration, self-control, psychic balance. Lacking a moral center, overtaken by the sensual fever of sheer consciousness, he is impelled to experiment cruelly on his wife's feelings. Like Saul in this respect, Candaules values more his complexity rather than his moral obligations. This attitude, of course, emanates from Gide's conviction that true personality lies in the acceptance of one's idiosyncracy or anomaly. Candaules not only accepts his idiosyncracy but also imposes it on others at the expense of his life. If Candaules' experiment is the expression of a creative unrest, no wonder that in the aesthetic exultation over his wife's beauty, the artist-king has altogether lost the natural jealousy of the lover. What would, indeed, account for his bizarre impulse to share his wife with Gyges?

Of Candaules' malaise, many diagnoses have been offered. His voluntary sharing of his wife is usually thought of as a sexual perversion. Exemplifying the "bestowing virtue of Zarathustra," Candaules' act, which transcends the conventional judgement of good and evil, testifies to his self-surpassing. Like Philoctetes, Candaules yields his most precious possession and, now freed from all appearances and pretense, attains being. This problem of *being* and *appearance* underlies the argument of all Gide's plays. In this context, being is sincerity to oneself, opposed to morality which, to Gide, is only social hypocrisy. Cooperating with the tragic operations of his nature, Candaules then tries to reconcile sincerity and morality in his experiment. If he achieves

40

anything, it is the exhibition of his sublime heroism. With this "quasi-mystical dilation of feeling" goes the disintegration of his moral faculties. Hence he shows no strong resistance to the imperious urges of his nature. Consequently he considers himself responsible to no one else but an inner god. However, equal to this tragic destiny, Candaules is fully conscious of his decisions and actions. Because of the bold originality of his experiment, he deliberately risks his universal good fortune, his wife, his life, without any sense of shame. Even the mere realization that he harbors such a daring idea entices him to action. Thus he asks himself: "Who else will ever do it if not thou?" His intensely introspective mind then discovers the roots of the absurd. In Gyges he finds a friend who, by seducing the queen, could calm the tumult of his generous nature. His "giving nature," his idiosyncracy, is Candaules' tragic fault. In fulfilling his nature, which is inherently complicated, Candaules brings about his doom.

According to Gide's preface to his play, everything that Candaules does is natural. Precisely in following his natural self, he becomes exceptional. Gide further believes that all possible feelings exist in man. Aware that any applause to a dramatic performance of his play will be an inevitable misunderstanding, he declares that besides its deeper meaning, a dramatic work should be a "fine spectacle": that the dramatist "should not fear to speak to the senses." Of Candaules' wish to exhibit the queen naked, Gide says: "Speech makes less impression than the sight of things." If he says that "Ideas are the skeleton of my drama," he nevertheless warns us: "let no one look for 'symbols' here, but simply for an occasion to generalize. And may the choice of such a subject, the exceptional character of Candaules, find in the play its explanation and excuse." Ideas, like history or legend, serve beauty if they reflect the uniqueness of the individual. Using no technique or lyrical overloading or bombast, he aspires for logic and severe probity: a cold, rapid, inelastic drawing. Gide exhibits here the classic purity of a tragic action which passes from recognition and discovery to the turn of fortune and the downfall of the protagonist. With full consciousness of his inevitable plight, Candaules yields to the force of his absolute sincerity. Freeing himself from his attachments, he resolves his search for identity: "Hide close! It's mad, the thing I am about to do. Speak louder, my youngest thought! Where do you mean to lead me?" Yet he cannot hold back. Leading the invisible Gyges into the queen's bedroom, Candaules bears the ordeal, experiencing no remorse at all. In fact, his dying words affirm his responsibility for all: "Gyges, I gave you the knife too." Throughout the play, Candaules remains his natural and authentic self.

What reveals the inner nature of Candaules is, on the whole, the force of his own designs. While believing that "the only exquisite emotion is surprise," he confesses that he does not know what his happiness is, assuring us that we feel it "only when we are not looking for it." Eventually the oracle of the magical ring comes true—but only with Candaules' complicity. With the "experiment" occurring inside the palace, our attention is focused on the spiritual dilemma of both Gyges and Candaules. To tie up the king's inner struggle with the outside world over which he rules, Philebus is made to narrate the interior happenings to the courtiers. This underlines the fact that the king's private acts produce reverberations throughout his kingdom. Because of the magnitude of his person, his fall affects the whole society. With pity we are drawn to the anguished Candaules, but with terror we are repelled by his masochistic exploit. On the other hand, Gyges agonizes for his violation of the queen, fighting off his remorseful conscience. A pitiable victim of his simplicity, he implores the king to hide him from the crime of his heart. Gyges' simplicity presents easily a direct contrast to Candaules' complexity. But what is Candaules striving for? Nothing else but the attainment of sincerity. Had he not challenged his flatterers to reveal their true natures in drunkenness? What the play renders immediate is Candaules' search for self-unity. Discovering and expressing aspects of himself, he finally accepts death. True to his affections up to the end, he apprehends and welcomes the fate that is the fruit of his will.

Many critics have underscored, particularly in Candaules' experiment, the communistic orientation of this play. Others have argued that, although it may not be wholly anti-capitalistic in its "message," its humoristic theme is perfectly compatible with communist ideology. Such interpretations are obviously tendentious. For art is definitely not propaganda in its total form. However that may be, it is revealing to note how Gide recasts the Greek myth, which originates from Herodotus, to dramatize his individualism. In stressing the positive role of Candaules, endowed with his peculiar attitude and mode of being, Gide has assigned him a central role in the drama. Whereas Nyssia and Gyges are only given typifying qualities (e.g., her beauty, his poverty), Candaules' moods and attitudes are fully delineated in gesture and behavior. For background, comic relief, and social setting, Gide introduces the courtiers who represent the spirit of conformity. When the courtiers salute Gyges as the new king, we observe that they serve merely as types, continuing through history as surviving witnesses of order and tradition. As soon as Gyges orders Nyssia to put on her veil again, the ancient order of things is restored. Both Gyges and the queen affirm the selfish quality of happiness. At this point, we are back at the beginning of the play, at the moment when Candaules would keep the queen for himself alone.

We may finally construe the conflict between Gyges and Candaules as the opposition, in allegorical terms, between brute instinct and refined sensibility. Of course Gide urges his readers beforehand not to look for symbols. Moreover, he characterized this play as "an invitation to generalization." But what is generalization if not some mode of allegory? We can speculate further on the metaphysical implications of Candaules' deed. However, it is sufficient to point out that his experiment, sublime and perverse at the same time, realizes his idea of moral liberty and of sincerity to the self as a ruling ethic. In this context, sincerity means one's faithful manifestation of what is unique in himself. Whatever is unique, be it good or evil, pleasant or painful, one must manifest, for that is the duty of the individual to himself. Gide's central principle of individual uniqueness as a value in itself is rendered here in the powerful characterization, through a swiftly evolving dramatic action, of Candaules' exemplary identity.

---

[1] Gide says:" . . . the eagle consumes us, vice or virtue, duty or passion," in *Prometheus Misbound* (New Directions Book, 1943), p. 145.

[2] Lawrence Thomas, *André Gide: The Ethic ot the Artist* (London, 1950), pp. 124-125.

VI

BATHSHEBA:
THE PLEASURE OF
CONTRADICTION

Bathsheba illustrates, in the person of King David, how desires are the true gods of men, how they mysteriously influence man's destiny. Gide believes that behind each of our desires lurks hidden a god; gods are immanent in all our desires. With the multiplicity of desires exists a plurality of gods. Each of our instincts exerts a force equal to the others so that human actions escape the control of the will. In a man's perplexity about the object of his desires, he commits gratuitous deeds whose justification lies in his implacable uncertainty. Thus the dove in this play, symbolic of the spirit of grace, leads David to yield to carnal desires. As the ambiguous symbol of nature also, the dove brings about David's sin, his downfall and repentance. When David in the first scene harps on the fact that "without God, even the strong man faileth," he unknowingly forecasts his downfall. Actually David's waywardness is of an intricately moral kind. It involves the traditional conflict between the spirit and the flesh, the self's passion and the tribal law.

In David's prayer the theme of the hero in quest of self-definition exposes itself as embodied in the pattern of impulse, deed, and guilt. Unveiling before us the dualism between body and soul, David's struggle, his existential *agon* which constitutes the dramatic predicament, is projected as a tension of conflicting values. Ultimately David's obsession unfolds itself as an inquiry concerning his authentic self.

Like Saul, David at the outset finds that he has lost communion with God. He arrives at the edge of an abyss and enters the dark night of the soul in which he presses the name of God to his lips "as a mother presses her dear child in her arms." Since grace is wanting, David must act alone, conscious of his vacillations, his timorous frailty. He pursues the dove of the Absolute, of ideal virtue: "To whatever place you mount, O dove, there I shall wait." David assumes a passive, receptive stance. When the dove descends and becomes incarnate in the voluptuous shape of Bathsheba, flesh and spirit coalesce. David discovers Bathsheba bathing in a fountain where the dove vanished; the site becomes an emblem of life, instinctive strength, virginity. To attain selfhood is, for David, to possess Bathsheba: metonymy becomes metaphor. To possess the flesh of the woman is to fuse with God—such is the logical step in resolving David's predicament.

In the first scene, David sets down his esteem for, and gratitude to, Uriah who—David informs us—saved his life once. When he seduces Uriah's wife later, he violates his own pledge of gratitude. In effect David travesties his own honor. Such a deed is already prefigured by David's fear of the prophet Nathan, the friend of Uriah. Nathan may be construed here as a projection of David's conscience. David's personality attempts to mediate between this moral voice (the internalized patriarchal authority) and the power of his libidinal energies. Juxtaposed with David's fluid character, Joab is the character type who heightens by contrast the round, multi-faceted figure of David. Profoundly aware of human fallibility, David strives to commune with God—but to no avail. In contrast, Joab as the obedient subject of David escapes the tangle of David's spiritual instability. His inertness associated with his servility seems to reflect the peace desired by David. Like Joab, Uriah plays the role of the responsible and devoted subject. Ashamed of his unfinished duty in the siege of Rabah, he refuses the invitation of David. His character acquires a fixed immediacy in David's recollections. Toward

David Uriah shows an attitude of respect, of unquestioning loyalty. All the ties between Uriah and David are given in retrospect through David's monologue. Evidently the play concerns itself with the character of David who, as king, represents the noble selflessness of which man is capable; as a human being, he epitomizes the common weakness of mortals.

In Scene II, we meet David describing his encounter with Bathsheba. Joab acts as one-man audience sustaining the continuity of David's thoughts with his provocative questions. Joab's primary function here is to connect David's solitary self, exiled from society by reason of kinghood and priesthood, with the outside world of temptations over which he claims to rule. (Significantly, David's garment, described as "Half-priestly, half warlike garb," suggests his role as a pilgrim-fighter: wrestling with the flesh to conquer spiritual beatitude, acting to attain an actionless stasis.) Such a link between David's self and the world is also established when the dove of his vision merges with Bathsheba's nude figure. David is compelled not only by his gratitude to Uriah to go out of his "cloister" and mingle with the world—indeed, he performs a gesture of *noblesse oblige*. He transcends his own self in search of the dove, now transfigured into Uriah's wife, whom he must subdue in the flesh if he is to attain unity or integrity of self and dissolve the affliction of heterogeneity. Would this imply that God can be known and is known only through the indulgence of the flesh? Would this dramatic turn imply that to fulfill our passion is to enter the state of grace? Gide's moral experiment finds its most seductive figure here.

When Gide transforms the dove of the spirit into Bathsheba's shape, we recall one observation of his: "Pagans rarely considered qualities of the soul as goods that could be acquired, but rather as natural properties like those of the body." David himself reconciles the senses and the spirit with his bacchic rapture. He speaks of the wine's effect: "It filled my heart like the fulfillment of prayer, I felt the strength of my loins renewed." Recalling the water with which Uriah saved David's life, wine here betokens absolution. It suggests the purification of the body and rebirth of the soul.

47

While Bathsheba's body is portrayed as a bizarre and mysterious shape, the spirit of God incarnates itself in the bird apprehended through the senses. The ambiguity is sublimated in the love-act which becomes here a ceremony of sacrifice. Confessing his weakness to the demands of his erotic urge, David submits with full consciousness: "But desire, Joab, desire enters the soul like a hungry stranger." However, his thirst cannot be quenched by the "littleness" of Uriah's happiness: "How could I ever possess little enough? All would be well if I desired nothing but her; but—" Whence comes the mood of perturbation? Once more Uriah has pledged himself to David as Lord of Israel. While Uriah besieges the gates of the enemy, David "besieges" Bathsheba's body to possess God. And even as Uriah is betrayed and killed at the instigation of David, so David betrays himself into believing that Bathsheba is the answer to the mystery of his unrest.

After having seduced Bathsheba, David realizes his self-deception—or, from another perspective, God's playfulness. Like the spiritual plague which tormented Saul his predecessor, David's anxiety cannot find adequate objectification as though it arose from a primordial trauma. Provoked by no known stimulus and engendered from within, such anxiety springs from the Faustian striving of finite man for the infinite, for a missing complementary Other. David remembers Saul's predicament: "The Lord no longer listens to me; no longer speaks through my mouth, no longer speaks to me." Note here the conception of God as a power within as well as without David's self. Ultimately David's project is to reconcile the god within (his desire) and the god without (Bathsheba), the woman serving as the temporary objectification of his desire.

One observes David's inner motivation from his statement: "But lately I can hardly bear His silence. I will force Him to speak." In Act III, David manifests his fear of Nathan the prophet. In effect, his double (the priest as super-ego) asserts himself and intensifies his guilt. Curiously enough he achieves a tone of detachment as he examines his conscience:

An act in the light of the sun, to the eyes of the flesh, may seem
beautiful
But woe to him who in darkness looks back with the eyes of the
spirit!
Woe to him who may not sleep at the top of an action done . . . .
But in darkness endlessly call it to mind,
As a blind man caresses with his hands to recognize
The face of a dead friend whom he loved.

Although this accuser in his dream overtakes David's
daylight self and indicts his worldly acts, David still justifies
his yielding to desire: "But now I ask God, what can a man do
if behind every one of his desires God is hidden? He pleads for
a recognition of his virtuous intent. Nevertheless Nathan
emerges in his mind to judge his deed. Later David admits his
guilt, confessing bitterly that he "did not know how to feed my
desire." His desires being by definition insatiable, David's
seduction of Bathsheba proves purposeless—an ironically
gratuitous act. Consequently he refuses to accept the reality of
his deed. Mimicking an act of repentance, he discloses the
truth of his psyche: seeing Bathsheba in mourning, he cries
out: "I hate her!" Could it be that in leaving David's desire
unattached, God (incarnate in Bathsheba) has pronounced a
verdict on David's deed? It seems that so long as man of blood
and flesh is afflicted by the desire to be one with the Absolute,
so long will he fail in his attempt to reach the stage of classic
repose: the synthesis of intellect and emotion, the harmony of
intention and deed. Such is the case with David. What he has
ecstatically yearned to possess becomes, after the possession, an
object of repulsion. Life becomes an interminable dialectical
process between the finite self and the infinite deity it projects
from within or without.

As soon as David loses himself in the thrall of his
passions, he is tormented with a sense of having been deluded
by his desires, his gods. Though he possesses Bathsheba, the
Absolute still eludes him. It flees from the illusory appearance
by which it has momentarily disclosed itself. David's
experience focuses this problem: "When at last, Joab, I held
her in my arms, would you believe it, I almost doubted
whether it were she I desired, or whether it was not perhaps

49

the garden . . . or the wine . . . " Caught in the flux of passion, David loses psychic equilibrium. Could it be that the object of his thirst is an idea of tranquil simplicity, an image of self-sufficiency coeval with death? If Bathsheba is not enough, what could satisfy David? With his "despotic reason," Nathan the prophet and his parable points out the falsity of his carnal passion. Though David might yield to each of his master-passions, he remains restless. (However, in his lyrical frenzy, the crudity of his lust disappears.) A spiritual bliss seems to characterize his dispossession when he cries out: "What can a man do if behind every one of his desires God is hidden?" Indeed, for Gide, "desires are true gods so long as they rule." Moreover, "It was not by free choice that man devoted himself to a particular god; the gods recognized their own image in the man." Each god in the pantheon of classical antiquity corresponds to each of the human instincts. Upholding the unquenchable appetite of his spirit, David recoils from Bathsheba. Could it be that his hatred or disgust is but a symptom of his striving for the Absolute? The recurrent theme in this play can be formulated by one of Gide's aphorisms: "In any case, the eagle consumes us, vice or virtue, duty or passion"—the eagle here referring to the vultures that punished Prometheus.

The dithyrambic tone of David's speeches in this play reflects the movement of his mind in aspiring towards union with the Absolute, the "God" of fulfilled desires. It signifies the possible liberation of David's spirit from the crude and tangible world of things that can be possessed. What the play essentially presents is the spiritual drama of David's self unfolding in the act of recollection. With the past as the subject of meditation, David is able to observe and judge himself with a measure of objectivity, as if his image in memory were someone else's. In the beginning, David's prayer foreshadows the subsequent vissicitudes of the theme of desire. Overwhelmed by doubts and anxiety, he annuls his testimony of debt to Uriah, seduces Bathsheba, and afterwards suffers remorse. Like Oedipus he can know himself only through an ordeal; but unlike Oedipus, David's ordeal involves not fate but his passions. There seems to be no explicit accounting for the *donée* of the play: the enigmatic unrest of his spirit, the inward uncertainty that controls the convergence of circumstances in David's predicament. But although David occupies the foreground, it is Bathsheba as the symbol of what devours him who emerges as the real subject of meditation. For she not only guides and directs the movement of David's mind, she also reveals the inescapable ambiguity of human desire and generates the epiphany of David's true self. The truth of the self, -however, remains a suspended question thrown to the audience.

VII

PERSEPHONE: SEDUCTIONS OF THE UNDERWORLD

The dialectics of death and life, renunciation and possession, finds its most moving poetic rendition in this play. Essentially a ritual re-organization of the Greek myth, Gide's version envisages the cycle of the seasons as the overarching pattern or macrocosm informing the vicissitudes of human passion. What attracted Gide to this fable of the Divine or Primordial Maiden—the combined Mother-Daughter archetype—is its theme of suffering, death/renunciation and rebirth. Distilling from the myth a personal allegory, Gide interprets the legend in the light of the Christian concept of redemption through self-sacrifice. Thus Persephone, with generous compassion for destitute humanity, abandons her security and peace to bring daylight to the shadowy underworld of suffering shades. Moved by pity at the sight of human distress, she descends of her own will to the realm of Pluto to assuage the pain of the multitude.

In his reconstruction of the myth, Robert Graves points out that Persephone (from *phero* and *phonos*, "she who brings destruction") and her abduction may be read as an allegorical translation of the historic usurpation of the female agricultural mysteries by patriarchal power in primitive times. On the whole, Graves believes that the symbolic meaning of Persephone, or Kore, cannot be divorced from the celebration of Demeter as the goddess of the cornfield, the intiator of brides and bridegrooms to the mystery of erotic bliss.[1] While

Hades (which stands for the Hellenic concept of the ineluctability of death) succeeds in kidnapping Persephone in the act of picking flowers in a meadow at Eleusis, her eating of the pomegranate in the underworld has been read as analogous to Sheol, goddess of Hell, devouring Tammuz in the fertility myth of adjacent cultures. Persephone's absence equals her mother Demeter's curse imposed on earth, but her restoration stands for the pre-Hellenic hope of regeneration, the promise of resurrection after death. Demeter herself contains the three phases or moments of life differentiated into Kore (the green corn), Persephone (the ripe ear) and Hecate (the harvested corn)—the cycle of organic, corporeal existence.

Critics have seen in this transformation theme of the myth Gide's preoccupation with social questions. The drama's parable has been construed as a vehicle for delivering Gide's communist ideal. It was during the composition of this play that Gide's consciousness was preoccupied with the necessity of negating private property; a recent visit to the coal mines where workers lived like prisoners in Pluto's Hades seems to be the probable inspiration for this almost transparent appeal for the redemption of the underworld toilers. Persephone apostrophizes her mother trying to make a god out of the mortal infant Demophoon, "the one hope of my heart!/Shall I, through you, look on the earth again/In flower? You must teach mankind to till/The fields, as Mother once taught you." Eumolpe declares that human labor "shall bring back Persephone/to love, to light, to life." In his contribution to *The God That Failed*, Gide recounts the failure of Demeter to transform the infant Demophoon into a god: "Metaneira, the mother—so the legend relates—anxious for the safety of her child, burst one night into the room, and, thrusting aside the goddess, scattered the embers with all the superhuman virtues which were being wrought and, in order to save the child, sacrificed the god."[2] Thus, three years after celebrating Persephone/Demeter, Gide in 1936 refuses the transcendence of a cosmic vision for the pathos of the human.

We may take two symbols, the narcissus and the pomegranate, to unlock the figurative design of the play.

While the narcissus flower connotes self-sufficiency, the pomegranate suggests the sensual pleasures of the daylight world. By gazing into the narcissus, a mirror of her desires, Persephone sees revealed there not herself but the underworld: suffering, loss of identity, death. Likewise Gide the artist, in gazing into himself, perceives the need for a social revolution, a profound change of one's character and position in life. Happiness, for Gide, no longer lies in eating the pomegranate, the fruit of the earth, to gratify one's self-indulgence; he refuses Persephone's gesture. Human happiness is found not in freedom, it appears, but in the acceptance of a duty, a heroic act in itself. But Persephone, instead of being forced by Hades, willingly descends to the underworld as though offering her services for a humanitarian cause. She is compelled not by an external law or will but by her love. Her mission is to bring poetry to the sufferers—a role which suggests Orpheus' deed of employing the power of art to diminish suffering and resurrect the dead. Through the narcissus-mirror of his own conscience, Gide forsakes his cherished aesthetic ideal of disinterestedness, of the detached gratuitous act, and resolves to dedicate himself to the welfare of others.

Besides being emblematic of self-love, the narcissus functions also as a concrete signifier of Persephone's spiritual beauty and its ephemeral quality. Ephemeral too is the love/pleasure associated with her mother Demeter. Attracted to the narcissus, Persephone is drawn toward the inevitable destiny of all creation subject to time. It seems that the ascendancy of Demeter is temporary. On the other hand, the Danaides represent the dimension of an eternal reality which assigns to mortal things their purpose in the cosmic scheme. Perpetually drawing water from the river of life, they proclaim: "We have no destiny/But again and again/To make the meaningless gesture of life." In this repeated gesture is crystallized the archetypal pattern of death and rebirth which the structure of the myth incorporates.

In a seminal analysis of the Kore figure in mythology, the scholar C. Kerenyi expounds on the philosophical meaning of the twin figure of Demeter/Persephone which clarifies Gide's aesthetic project:

> Mother divided from daughter, and the mown ear, are two symbols of something unspeakably painful that is hidden in the Demeter-aspect of the world; but also of something very consoling . . . . The grain-figure is essentially the figure of both origin and end, of mother and daughter; and just because of that it points beyond the individual to the universal and eternal. It is always *the grain* that sinks to earth and returns, always the grain that is mown down in golden fullness, and yet, as fat and healthy seed, remains whole, mother and daughter in one. [Note how the grain which dies gives birth, its thematic import, is replicated in Gide's motto "If it die . . ." from John, 12:24.] The idea of the original Mother-Daughter goddess, at root a single entity, is at the same time the idea of *rebirth*.
>
> To enter into the figure of Demeter means to be pursued, to be robbed, raped, to fail to understand, to rage and grieve, but then to get everything back and be born again. And what does all this mean, save to realize the universal principle of life, the fate of everything mortal? What, then, is left over for the figure of Persephone? Beyond question, that which constitutes the structure of the living creature *apart from* this endlessly repeated drama of coming-to-be and passing-away, namely the *uniqueness* of the individual and its *enthralment to non-being*. Uniqueness and non-being understood not philosophically but envisaged corporeally in figures, or rather as these are envisaged in the formless, unsubstantial realm of Hades. There Persephone reigns, the eternally unique one who is no more.[3]

Punctuated by its transitoriness, Persephone's beauty is defined precisely by its momentary presence, glimpsed at the instant of its evanescence.

Gide shares with Keats and Novalis the romantic sensibility of conceiving beauty and death together, grief being the chord which accompanies the knowledge that beauty doesn't endure. Gazing at the narcissus, Persephone experiences the chilling desolation of winter as it shrouds the earth. It is Mercury (symbolizing the flux of existence) who gives her the pomegranate. He is pursued by the Hours personifying the passage of time. Meanwhile, in her wanderings and search for her daughter (her self doubled), Demeter assumes her maternal status. While Persephone lies "dead" in the underworld, Demophoon grows up, soon to be claimed by her as mate as soon as the earth flowers again in abundant harvest. With the sentiment of love is attached an erotic element counterpointing decay and death. This balance prefigures the rythm of the seasons, the cycle of organic life. More than once does Persephone emphasize the overbearing force of destiny as witnessed in nature itself. Such a destiny informs Persephone's unsolicited love for afflicted humanity. Having perceived the painful truth of human suffering, she descants:

Henceforth how could I
Heedlessly laugh and sing with you,
Now that I have seen, now that I know.
How a thwarted multitude suffers
And waits endlessly.
O piteous host of shades, you beckon me.
Toward you I go . . . .

Thus we see that as soon as Persephone plucks the narcissus, she coalesces with its fate. The object of her love, which the flower incarnates in its beauty, is death; the abyss of non-being seduces her. Her love for the suffering, the victim, is an acceptance of her destiny. Beauty and self-sacrifice co-exist. Is Persephone annihilated by her desire? Although the nymphs admonish her not to follow her love too hard, she renounces Demophoon, her earthly love, and plunges into Hades. In the underworld, however, through the narcissus (her double) she can share in earthly life above, in much the same way that on

57

earth she can participate in the agonies of the world below. This perfectly mirrors Gide's ambivalence, his duplicity (his passion for counterfeiting "the real" in the imaginary sphere), his passion for alternating or varying masks, personae, roles. The play indeed captures the Gidean drama of heroic assertion through renunciation.

In this operatic drama enacted in four scenes, Gide employs songs, choral ballet, mime, and lyrical prose as elements of a symbolic theater reminiscent of Maeterlinck and Yeats' plays. Gide's verse has been described as an accomplished mixture of diluted Racine and Valery, quite appropriate to the modernized Gluck of Stravinsky's setting.[4] While the dance movements create an aura of ritual enacting the myth, the music aims to project the passage of feelings in the characters. Analogous to meter and rhyme, the orchestral accompaniment transposes into chords and tones the predominant mood of anxiety or of rapture in each tableau. For narrator Gide employs a chorus leader Eumolpe who, at the beginning of each scene, sums up the action of each episode so that an epic-like narrative effect is produced. He also interprets to the audience the mimetic gestures of the characters, thus generating aesthetic distance.

Oscillating between rapture and grief, Persephone's experience captures the theme invested in the four tableaux: "For Spring to be reborn/The seed must consent to go/Underground and die/So it may come up again/The future's golden grain." In essence, Gide again celebrates the enigmatic paradox of presence in absence, reinventing the heroic by transcending the received or ordained hero.[5]

---

[1] *Greek Myths* (London, 1958), pp. 89-90, 93, 95-96, 123.

[2] *The God That Failed*, pp. 157-158.

[3] C. G. Jung and Carl Kerenyi, *Essays on a Science of Mythology* (New York, 1963), pp. 117, 123-124. For supplementary insights, see Mircea Eliade, *Myths, Dreams and Mysteries* (New York, 1960), pp. 155-189.

[4] G. D. Painter, *André Gide* (London, 1952), p. 162.

[5] This central thematic design of Gide's art and life epitomized in this play, the paradigm of his Weltanschauung, is lucidly formulated in two pages by

Martin Turnell, *The Art of French Fiction* (New York, 1959), pp. 283-284. For further reflections on the notion of the modern hero *vis-à-vis* Gide's peculiar synthesis, compare those in the collection *The Hero in Literature*, ed. Victor Brombert (Greenwich, Connecticut, 1965), pp. 265-282.

CONCLUSION

In Goethe's *Faust*, after the wager contracted with
Mephistopheles and an impassioned outburst of desire to
absorb all possible experience, Faust interrupts the Spirit of
Negation's skeptical deflation of his rapture: "Alas, what am I,
if I can/Not reach for mankind's crown which merely
mocks/Our senses' craving like a star?" Mephistopheles
cryptically answers: "You're in the end—just what you are!"[1]
About a hundred years later, Nietzsche's Zarathustra arrives
at the discovery of Mephistopheles' meaning: " . . . in the end,
one experiences only oneself. The time is gone when mere
accidents could still happen to me; and what could still come
to me now that was not mine already? What returns, what
finally comes home to me, is my own self and what of myself
has long been in strange lands and scattered among all things
and accidents."[2] Could we say that Gide's all-embracing project
to shape the curve of his life as an art-work is to reaffirm the
truth of Zarathustra's insight and to dramatize its moral
vicissitudes? Underlying the multiple, exuberant masks of his
empathies lies an evangelical egotism that takes pleasure in
always negating and compromising itself.

The "self," for Gide, however, cannot be defined once
and for all in a constative or propositional form with a
referential guarantee since it is less a concept than an
imperative. In his early "Narcissus," Gide expresses
dissatisfaction with a contemplative and solipsistic attitude:
"—but what does he know of his power as long as it remains
unaffirmed? By dint of gazing at them, he cannot distinguish
himself from those things; not to know where one ends—not
to know how far one reaches?"[3] Just as Faust exhorted his
generation to strive daily in order to deserve freedom and

61

conquer beauty, the artist of "Narcissus" points out that "Paradise has always to be remade; it is not in some *ultima thule*."[4] The integrity of Gide's "self" is then equivalent to an endless, compulsive process of making and unmaking impelled by a self-willed fatality, a sequence of actions, gestures, speech-acts and discourses in the performative mode. What has perpetually scandalized people about Gide's supple, reflexive stance is its capacity to sustain its lucid and impassioned obsession with the contradictory possibilities of any action or situation. Gide defies any systematizing tendency that suppresses those possibilities by the force of a radical skepticism, almost an anarchic flexibility that manages to contrive fantastic games of substitutions, alternating perspectives, extrapolations. In such games he hopes to be faithful to the gratuitous flux and oscillations of his temperament. In a commentary alluded to earlier, Roland Barthes astutely deciphers the Gidean signature inscribed in the uncanny subterfuges and craftiness of his writing: "This fidelity to the truth of his life is heroic." What, then, is the "truth" whose seductiveness inaugurates the exceptional?

Nothing more nakedly confessional can adumbrate that truth than this statement of what Gide endeavors to typify in his protagonists, namely, the oxymoronic and ambiguous sensibility of a psyche constituted by an incessant process of affirming and negating:

> I have never been able to renounce anything; and protecting in my self both the best and the worst, I have lived as a man torn asunder. But how can it be explained that this cohabitation of extremes in me led not so much to restlessness and suffering as to a pathetic intensification of the sentiment of existence, of life? The most opposite tendencies never succeded in making me a tormented person; but made me rather perplexed—for torment accompanies a state one longs to get away from, and I did not long to escape what brought into operation all the potentialities of my being. That state of dialogue which, for so many others, is almost intolerable became necessary to me. This is also because, for those others, it can only be injurious to action, whereas for me, far from leading to sterility, it invited me to

62

the work of art and immediately preceded creation, it led to equilibrium and harmony.[5]

Gide further suggests that his character is one in which the expenditure of passion does not exhaust but renews, so that this belief in the prolific novelty of actions and the utopian horizon of the future prevents him from investing libidinal energy in eternal life. Immortality for him "is that almost perfect satisfaction I enjoy in effort itself and in the immediate realizing of happiness and harmony."[6]

The dialectical imagination exercised by Gide in his plays operates mainly to contextualize the impulse to incarnate the authentic which he once identified with the gratuitous act—the unmotivated and uncalled-for gesture of pure bravura which explodes traditional codes, sanctions, authorities. Site of the self-deconstructing genius, the gratuitous act of his typical protagonists epitomizes the Gidean virtue of the reckless adventure into the unknown, the realm of genuine freedom. But this blind and empty freedom can be sustained only in thought, not in concrete experience. There is the facticity of bodies and reified rituals to reckon with. Hence the obsession with scruples and the discrimination of nuances, the foregrounding of incommensurably equivocal positions. Gide rejoices in the adventure of the search, in the sheer pleasure of fabricating or discovering something new: "How easy it is to work according to an aesthetic and a morality already given! Writers who are submissive to a recognized religion advance with the confidence of a sure thing. I have to invent all. Sometimes it is an immense groping toward an almost imperceptible light. And sometimes I wonder: what for?"[7] In contrast to the universalizing or essentializing drive of New Critical formalism, or even modernist structuralism, Gide provokes not in order to moralize on the "eternal verities" but to call attention to the present: "What Sophocles was unable to see and understand, though offered by his subject" is what Gide is trying to present, "not because I am more intelligent, but because I belong to another age . . and it is to your intelligence that I address myself."

63

One can argue that Gide's theater is an attempt to transcend the anonymous, consumerized and depersonalized character of mass society surrounding it by insisting on the artifice of art, the perpetually unfixed, mutable protean nature of the illusion presented on stage. The thesis of his lecture "The Evolution of the Theater" precisely stressed a central theme informing such early works as "Narcissus": "All things have always existed in man, sometimes seen, more or less, and sometimes hidden; what in recent times has been discovered in him is newly disclosed to sight but had been there asleep in man from the beginning." [8] However, Gide is not nostalgic about origins. He polemicizes against Christianity for levelling individuals, destroying character, and imposing the "heroism of resignation, of acceptance." He upholds the plurality of the modern: a secular and contingent individualism redeemed by the imagination. Recognizing historical specificity and the determining limits of social contexts and symbolic regimes, Gide prophesies: "We expect of humanity new manifestations . . . " He invokes Nietzsche's image of the "heroic navigator" mapping forbidden territories and tabooed regions, exploring frontiers hitherto only dreamed or imagined.[9]

In *Bathsheba*, Gide puts these words into King David's mouth: "But now I ask God, Joab, what can man do/If behind every one of his desires God is hidden?" The signature of the Gidean is marked here in the rhetorical tautology where "God" is hidden, an immanent force masquerading in human desires, sheer movement or metamorphosis from the finite to the infinite, with "Joab" as a pretext, a mirroring witness. When Bathsheba is brought to David as a response to his "thirst" for God, he recoils at the consequence of his desire: the sacrifice of her husband Uriah, his faithful soldier. Despite the surface act of turning away from Bathsheba, the emblem of a Gidean "spirit of Negation," this Faustian pioneer of consciousness demonstrates the perverse replication of desire (in what Lacan calls the Imaginary sphere) when it re-enacts its own fertile misrecognition of its object. Actually, for Gide, desire has no object but its own self-exhibition, its refusal to be circumscribed by the Symbolic order founded on the law of the phallus, the Oedipal castration trauma. Pursuing this enterprise of re-inventing the heroic (in contrast to the hypostatized "hero"), Gide has fashioned a set of guidelines opposed to what demarcates and limits. Its watchword is *disponibilité*, the susceptibility to all experience, the unrelenting divestment of all fixed assumptions through incessant self-questioning and interrogation of any established principle or axiom. In "The Return of the Prodigal," the ideal of spontaneous but rigorous honesty traverses the circuitous route of a dialectic between polarities through which most of the plays must go: fetishism of the intellect versus sensuality, hedonistic self-indulgence versus ascetic moral commitment, the Apollonian versus the Dionysian phase, the ambition to encompass everything versus the drive to sacrifice everything. Gide is nothing if not a partisan for the diverse, the unseizable mutations, the counterfeits of enigmatic appearances. He has resuscitated the spirit of Hegel's dialectic, recapitulating thereby the moral history of western culture from the classical pagan ethos to Christianity, from the Renaissance through the reformation to the modern. The argument of Gide's theater, the inspiration of his dramatized fables and allegories, inheres in this single-minded effort of staging this dialectic in the creation of characters whose *species-being* epitomizes the human gift of self-transcendence: transvaluing received social conventions, moral consensus, aesthetic codes. Perhaps Gide's project is too much for ordinary mortals, a strenuous, unprecedented quest transpiring in the gap between Everything and Nothing; if so, that is probably its permanent salutary worth.

---

1 Lines 1803-1806 of Part I, *Goethe's Faust*, tr. Walter Kaufmann (New York, 1961), p. 191.

2 *The Portable Nietzsche*, ed. Walter Kaufmann (New York, 1954), p. 264.

3 André Gide, *The Return of the Prodigal* (London, 1953), p. 8.

4 *Ibid.*, p. 10.

5 André Gide, *Madeleine* (New York, 1952), pp. 70-71.

6 *Ibid.*, see also *The Journals of André Gide*, tr. Justin O'Brian (New York, 1947), Vol. II, p. 343.

7 *The Journals*, entry for 29 July 1930.

8 *My Theater* (New York, 1952), p. 272.

9 For Gide's comments on Nietzsche, see *The André Gide Reader*, ed. David Littlejohn (New York, 1971), pp. 188-196.

Ames, Van Meter. *André Gide*. New York: New Directions, 1947.

Barthes, Roland. *A Barthes Reader*. New York: Hill and Wang, 1982.

Brachfeld, Georges. *André Gide and the Communist Temptation*. Geneva: Librairie E. Droz, 1959.

Brombert, Victor, ed. *The Hero in Literature*. Greenwich, CT: Fawcett, 1965.

Burke, Kenneth. *Counter-Statement*. Berkeley: UP of California, 1968.

Crossman, Richard H., ed. *The God that Failed*. New York: Bantam, 1950.

Delay, Jean. *The Youth of André Gide*. Chicago: UP of Chicago, 1963.

Gide, André. *The André Gide Reader*. Ed. David Littlejohn. New York: Knopf, 1971.

————. *The Journals of André Gide*. Ed. Justin O'Brien. New York: Knopf, 1951.

————. *Madeleine*. New York: Knopf, 1952.

————. *Marshlands* and *Prometheus Misbound*. Trans. George D. Painter. New York: New Directions, 1953.

————. *My Theater*. Trans. Jackson Mathews. New York: Knopf, 1952.

————. *Pretexts: Reflections on Literature and Morality*. New York: Books for Libraries P., 1959.

————. "The Return of the Prodigal Son." Trans. Wallace Fowlie. *The Norton Anthology of World Masterpieces*. Ed. Maynard Mack. New York: Norton, 1979. 1371-1384.

———— -Paul Valery. *Correspondence*. Paris: Gallimard, 1955.

Goethe, J. W. *Goethe's Faust*. Trans. Walter Kaufmann. New York: Doubleday, 1961.

Gramsci, Antonio. *Selections from Prison Notebooks*. New York: International, 1971.

Graves, Robert. *Greek Myths*. London: Cassell, 1958.

Guerard, Albert. *André Gide*. Cambridge, Mass.: Harvard UP, 1953.

Jung, Carl G. and Carl Kerenyi. *Essays on a Science of Mythology*. New York: Harper, 1963.

Maclaren, James Clark. *The Theater of André Gide*. Baltimore: Johns Hopkins UP, 1953.

Mann, Klaus. *André Gide and the Crisis of Modern Thought*. New York: Creative Age P., 1943.

Nietzsche, Friederich. *The Portable Nietszche*. Ed. Walter Kaufmann. New York: Viking, 1954.

O'Brien, Justin. *Portrait of André Gide: A Critical Study*. New York: Knopf, 1953.

Painter, George. *André Gide*. New York: A. Barker, 1951.

Sartre, Jean Paul. *Situations*. New York: Fawcett, 1966.

Thain, Aldyth. *André Gide's The Return of the Prodigal Son*. Logan: UP of Utah, 1960.

Thomas, Lawrence. *André Gide: The Ethic of the Artist*. London: Secker and Warburg, 1950.

Turnell, Martin. *The Art of French Fiction*. New York: New Directions, 1959.

ABOUT THE AUTHOR

Educated in the University of the Philippines and Harvard University, E. SAN JUAN, Jr. is at present professor of English and Comparative Literature at the University of Connecticut, Storrs. He has taught at the University of California, Brooklyn College, and the Inter-University Centre of Postgraduate Studies in Yugoslavia, His recent books are *Toward a People's Literature* (University of the Philippines Press) which won the Catholic Mass Media Award and the Manila Critics Circle Prize; and *Crisis in the Philippines: The Making of a Revolution* (Bergin & Garvey). His book on the works of the leading Filipino writer in English Nick Joaquin, entitled *Subversions of Desire*,will be released this year by Ateneo University Press and the University of Hawaii Press.

San Juan received a Fulbright-Hayes lectureship award for 1987-88. He is at present completing research on the production of colonial/Third World discourse and practice vis-à-vis Western post-structuralist critical theory. His writings have been translated into Russian, German, Japanese, Italian, and other languages.